WFH

WORKING FROM HOME

Everything You Should Know About Working From Home – Tips and Strategies for Success

MARK DAVIES

All rights reserved © 2021 by Mark Davies

...

ISBN: 978-1-915218-01-8
First Edition: October 2021

This book is copyright protected. It is only for personal use. You cannot amend, distribute, sell, use, quote, or paraphrase any part of this book's content without the author or publisher's consent. All pictures contained in this book come from the author's personal archive or copyright-free stock websites (Pixabay, Pexel, Freepix, Unsplash, StockSnap, etc.).

Disclaimer Notice:

Please note the information contained within this document is for educational and entertainment purposes only. All effort has been executed to present accurate, up-to-date, reliable, complete information. No warranties of any kind are declared or implied. Readers acknowledge that the author is not engaged in rendering legal, financial, medical or professional advice. The content within this book has been derived from various sources. Please consult a licensed professional before attempting any techniques outlined in this book.

By reading this document, the reader agrees that under no circumstances is the author responsible for any losses, direct or indirect, that are incurred due to the use of the information contained within this document, including, but not limited to, errors, omissions, or inaccuracies.

The trademarks used are without any consent, and the publication of the trademark is without permission or backing by the trademark owner. All trademarks and brands within this book are for clarifying purposes only and are owned by the owners themselves, not affiliated with this document.

TABLE OF CONTENTS

INTRODUCTION 1

THE PROS AND CONS OF WORKING FROM HOME 5

    A Short History of Remote Work 6

    The Benefits of Working From Home 8

    Drawbacks of Work From Home 15

    Distractions When You Work from Home (And How to Avoid Them!) 19

WORKING FROM HOME CAN SAVE YOU MONEY 25

    Costs of Commuting 26

    Clothes 30

    Eating Out 31

    Tax Breaks 32

    The Environment 32

    Time 33

    Tips to Better Manage Our Money 34

WORK FROM HOME HACKS 39

    Tips for Working From Home to Increase Productivity 40

    Soft Skills Remote Workers Need 51

    3 Steps to Cultivate Soft Skills 57

SETTING UP YOUR HOME WORKSPACE 61

    How to Set Up a Home Office 62

    Improve Your Internet Connection for Remote Working 70

    Remote Work Apps For Every Work-From-Home Professional 75

    Are You Ready to Simplify Your Remote Work? 93

WORK FROM HOME IDEAS 95

    Freelance Jobs to Do From Home... 96

    Tips for Landing a Work-From-Home Job 104

    Best Freelance Websites to Find Job................................ 106

    How to Ask Your Boss to Work From Home.................. 119

THE WORK-FROM-HOME MINDSET 123

    Shifting to a Remote Mindset 123

    Maintaining the Growth Mindset 129

    What are the Psychological Effects of Working from Home? 134

CONCLUSION 138

INTRODUCTION

Flexible work is the future of work. Working from home is increasingly trending and can be beneficial to both the employer and the employee. It has grown in popularity as an alternative to conventional office employment in recent years.

Work from home refers to work performed remotely rather than in an office. As a nickname for the concept, the acronym "WFH" is used. Telecommuting, Remote work, Working Remotely, and Virtual work are all synonyms for Work From Home.

Job has traditionally been performed in an office. Employees complete corporate operations and work-related activities in a physical workspace. With the advancement in digital transformation, this is changing. Companies are discovering that many of their workers are no longer constrained by a physical workspace to function effectively as technological capabilities become more complex and business processes depend on them more. Working from home or telecommuting can be just as effective.

Even before the global pandemic made working from home a temporary reality for millions, a growing number of people were saying farewell to their onerous commute to work. It's no longer important to be in an office full-time to be a productive member of the team, thanks to ever-evolving technology like Skype, Facetime, Slack, Zoom, Google Hangouts, authenticator software, and cloud storage, not to mention texting and email. Many types of work, in reality, can be performed just as effectively, if not more effectively, from a home office.

Remote work increased dramatically after the COVID-19 pandemic began. According to data compiled by the job search site FlexJobs, remote work will soon account for most of the workforce. Since the pandemic started, many businesses have already shifted to long-term remote work.

Suppose you want to start your own company to offer your services, skills, or goods, earn supplementary income as a freelancer, or work remotely full-time. In that case, there are more opportunities than ever to enter the work-from-home group. This book will first review the benefits (and drawbacks) of this new way of working. We'll uncover all the strategies and tips to be successful as a remote worker, what tools to use, and the correct mindset to be successful.

Next, we'll look at all the career choices and job opportunities that allow you to earn an income completely remotely. I will give some tips on finding remote work and suggestions on how to get hired for a work-from-home job.

THE PROS AND CONS OF WORKING FROM HOME

Suppose you are a home-based small business owner who works from home full-time or someone who divides his or her time by working from home on occasion. In that case, there is a range of advantages and disadvantages to consider when setting up a home office and planning your work environment. Since working out of a home-based office is certainly not for everyone, it's important to consider the many advantages and disadvantages before making it a part of your work process. After briefly reviewing the history of working from home, we'll look in detail at all the elements to help you decide if working from home is right for you.

A Short History of Remote Work

The introduction of work-from-home (WFH) policies in the 1970s, as soaring fuel prices triggered by the 1973 OPEC oil embargo made commuting more costly, arguably started a large-scale shift from conventional, colocated work to remote work. These policies encouraged people to work from home, in coworking spaces, or other community places such as coffee shops and public libraries on occasion, on a daily part-time basis, or full-time, to understand that they would return to the workplace regularly. Workers were often granted discretion over their schedules, enabling them to fit in school pickups, errands, or midday exercise without being seen as shirking. They saved time by driving less and took fewer sick days as a result.

WFH use grew in the 2000s due to the introduction of personal computers, the Internet, email, broadband access, smartphones, mobile phones, cloud computing, and videotelephony. This development was exacerbated by the need to comply with laws such as the Americans with Disabilities Act of 1990 and Equal Employment Opportunity Commission mandates.

Millennials were enthralled by the prospect of traveling the globe while still working.

According to research, there are efficiency advantages. According to a 2015 report, when workers opted into WFH policies, their productivity improved by 13%. When the same employees were given the option of staying at home or returning to the workplace nine months later, those who chose the former saw even greater gains: they were 22 percent more efficient than before the experiment. This implies that people should probably decide which situation (home or office) is best for them.

Many businesses have encouraged more workers to work from home in recent years. True, several major companies, including Yahoo and IBM, had reversed course before the pandemic, requesting that their workers resume colocated work in order to foster more productive cooperation. But other organizations moved toward greater geographic flexibility, allowing some if not all employees, new and old, to work from anywhere, completely untethered to an office.

Most companies that offer WFH options keep some workers at one or more offices. They are, in other words, hybrid-remote operations. However, Covid-19's forced experiment with all-remote work has prompted some of these companies to strategically shift toward majority-remote, with less than 50% of workers colocated in physical offices.

And before the recession, a small number of businesses had taken this practice a step further, closing down offices and dispersing everybody from entry-level associates to the CEO.

Though the pandemic may have prompted many millions of workers worldwide to work from home, it is far from the only explanation. Indeed, the advantages of working from home affect so many aspects on a global scale that it is almost certain to become the best way forward.

The Benefits of Working From Home

Remote work had a major moment when COVID-19 compelled businesses all over the world to send their workers home to work virtually.

Yes, several employers were caught off guard by the rush to provide workers with all of the resources they needed to work from home. However, after everyone had settled in, it became clear to many office-based teams that workers could be just as efficient and concentrated while they were not in the office—in many cases, even more so. Employers all over the world started to realize that remote work is a viable option.

A remote job, as we've long known, has a slew of benefits for employees. We've compiled a list of the best benefits of working from home, some of which you might already be aware of, and others that might open your eyes to the effect of remote work on employers, employees, the economy, and the environment.

1. Improved Work-Life Balance

Many remote jobs often have flexible hours, ensuring that employees can start and end their days whenever they want, as long as their work is completed and results in positive outcomes. When it comes to attending to your personal life needs, having leverage over your work schedule can be invaluable.

Dropping off kids at school, running errands, taking an online fitness class in the morning, or being home for a contractor are all easier to balance when you work from home.

2. Reduced Commute Stress

In the United States, the average one-way travel time is 27.1 minutes—nearly that's an hour per day spent driving to and from work, and it quickly adds up. According to the Auto Insurance Center, commuters spend about 100 hours a year driving and 41 hours stuck in traffic. Some "serious" commuters face 90-minute or longer commute times each way.

However, wasting time driving is just one to the drawbacks of going to and from work. More than 30 minutes of one-way commuting each day is associated with increased levels of stress and anxiety, and evidence indicates that commuting 10 miles to work each day is associated with health problems such as: • higher cholesterol • elevated blood sugar • increased risk of depression

By foregoing the commute, you can better maintain your mental and physical health. The time saved will allow you to concentrate on non-work priorities such as getting more sleep in the morning, spending more time with family, working out, or having a healthy breakfast.

3. Location Independence

One of the significant advantages of working from home is getting access to a wider variety of job opportunities that are not geographically restricted. This is particularly useful for job seekers who live in rural areas or small towns where there might not be many open local positions.

Since there is no fixed job site, completely remote employees may travel and live as digital nomads while maintaining a meaningful career before the pandemic. While a complete nomad lifestyle is currently on hold, it is still a distinct advantage as borders continue to open up.

People who must regularly relocate, such as military spouses, will profit from having a remote job that can be done from anywhere without starting from the ground floor of a new company with each transfer.

Furthermore, remote work is an excellent way to escape high-rent and high-mortgage areas, especially for positions (such as technology) that necessitate living in a city with a high cost of living. You don't have to live in a major metropolitan area with remote jobs to have a fulfilling career.

4. Increased Inclusivity

Remote work allows employers to promote diversity and inclusion by employing candidates from diverse social, ethnic, and cultural backgrounds and perspectives — something that can be difficult to do when recruitment is limited to a particular location that not everybody wants or can afford to live near.

Companies tend to embrace diversity, culture, and family by recruiting workers who can work from home in the neighborhoods where they feel most relaxed and valued.

People who may struggle to find stable employment at an onsite workplace, such as those with disabilities or caregivers who need a flexible schedule, may pursue their career aspirations without having to worry about commuting back and forth to an office. It also allows employees to travel to doctor's appointments and other healthcare appointments when required.

5. *Financial Savings*

People who work from home part-time will save about $4,000 a year. Gas, vehicle repairs, housing, parking fees, a professional wardrobe, purchased lunches, and other expenses may all be reduced or removed completely. These savings accumulate and put more money in your wallet.

And the savings aren't limited to workers. As more businesses, such as Twitter, Square, Shopify, and Facebook, encourage workers to work from home post-pandemic, they can see substantial long-term cost savings.

According to Global Workplace Analytics, an average organization will save approximately $11,000 per year for each employee who works from home at least part of the time. In reality, FlexJobs has saved over $5 million from remote work on items such as:

- Overhead
- Real estate costs
- Transit subsidies
- Operational continuity

Employers in the United States are saving more than $30 billion a day by encouraging workers to work from home during the COVID-19 pandemic. This significant economic benefit of remote work can continue as more businesses adopt it as a long-term solution.

6. Beneficial Environmental Impact

Before the pandemic, the 3.9 million workers who worked from home at least half the time lowered greenhouse gas emissions by the equivalent of taking over 600,000 vehicles off the road for an entire year. For those who work at least part-time from home, 7.8 billion car miles are avoided per year, 3 million tons of greenhouse gases (GHG) are avoided, and $980 million in oil savings are realized.

Remote employees will have the same effect on air quality as planting an entire forest of 91 million trees by making environmentally sound choices, including using less paper and controlling their air conditioning, heating, and lighting.

7. The Impact on Sustainability

Remote work contributes to a wide range of sustainability programs, including economic prosperity and reduced inequalities and sustainable cities, climate change, and responsible consumption.

Reduced commuting is one of the simplest and most cost-effective ways for businesses and workers to minimize their carbon footprint and impact climate change. In reality, the planet is already seeing significant reductions in emissions, congestion, and traffic due to the pandemic response, and being able to see the effects firsthand could be a driving force behind remote work for everyone involved.

8. A Workplace That Can Be Tailor-Made

A great advantage of remote work is the ability to set up a cozy home office. You can set up your home office and make it whatever you want, whether you just want a more ergonomic chair or you have health problems that necessitate specialized office equipment.

9. Improved Productivity and Performance

Working from home normally results in fewer interruptions, fewer office arguments, a lower noise level, and fewer (or more efficient) meetings. With no commute, remote workers usually have more time and fewer distractions, resulting in improved productivity — a significant advantage of working from home for both employees and employers.

When done correctly, remote work allows workers and businesses to concentrate on what really matters: results. Unfortunately, the workplace atmosphere will result in "false positives," which can contribute to prejudice and favoritism. After all, though arriving early and leaving late can appear to be more work, actual success is a much better measure of productivity.

According to FlexJobs' 2020 study, staff who believed they would be more productive working from home were actually more productive while working remotely.

During the pandemic, slightly more than half of the respondents (51%) said they are more active working from home. Many reported fewer interruptions and quieter work environments (68 percent for both) as contributing factors when asked why.

10. A More Fulfilling and Healthier Work Life

Remote, mobile staff are generally happier and more loyal employees, in part because working from home has been shown to reduce tension, provide more flexibility for hobbies and interests, and strengthen personal relationships, among other benefits.

Besides personal health and well-being, coworker and manager relationships can be more constructive without the distractions and politics of an in-office job. According to an estimated 72 percent of employers, remote work has a high effect on employee retention — in other words, workers are more likely to stay with their employer when they have remote work opportunities.

Working from home can also improve your health in many ways:

- More time for physical exercise
- Easier access to healthy foods
- Ability to recover from sickness or surgery at home;
- Reduced exposure to illnesses;
- Ease of caring for a health condition or disability;
- The ability to build a comfortable and ergonomic workspace.

Working from home will provide workers with the time and environment they need to make healthier decisions.

Drawbacks of Work From Home

If you enjoy or despise working from home, surveys show that it is here to stay for many businesses and employees. You may intend to make working from home a permanent, or at least an option, for your company's employees. And you might be intending to work from home indefinitely.

Since you've seen the advantages, here are some of the major disadvantages and what you can do with them.

1. Interruptions
You may encounter unwanted interruptions from your spouse, girlfriend, roommate, or children who don't fully comprehend that even though you're at home, you're still

working. Working at home when caring for small children is a special task that necessitates additional assistance from employers and other family members. When it comes to adults and older children in your home, it's up to you to set clear boundaries so that they know when it's appropriate to speak to you or invade your office and when it isn't. "Set aside 'do not disturb' hours that are free of interruptions," experts suggest.

2. *A 24-Hour Workday.*

You can feel obligated to make up for your absence from the office by being available 24 hours a day to do things like answer emails or solve problems. That's a specific issue for entrepreneurs who can't quickly turn off their job obligations. And, if your office is now in your living room or bedroom, it can be difficult to imagine yourself as being away from work.

But you must do so. You must withdraw fully from your job for a portion of each day and week, otherwise, your own results, mental and physical health, and, eventually, your business will suffer. If possible, separate your work space from your living space by placing it in a separate room or by erecting a screen. Make it clear to your clients, staff, and everyone else for whom you work that there will be periods that you will not respond to business demands.

3. *Fear of missing out (FOMO).*

One of the reasons so many of us overwork when we work from home is the fear of missing out. Even if everyone else in your organization is operating from home, it's difficult to escape the nagging feeling that there are things going on and discussions taking place that you should be aware of but aren't. If other people at your company are working in the office when you're working from home, the feeling can be much more intense — and research shows that people who work from home risk damaging their jobs in that case.

In any case, improved contact is the perfect antidote to FOMO. Pick up the phone and call a coworker or direct report to check-in or to say hello. Suppose you're curious about discussions or meetings that are taking place without your input. In that case, the easiest way is to ask your coworkers what's going on with important tasks or problems and if there are any important details you're lacking.

4. Never leaving the house.
Stay-at-home directives have been very literal for some of us. With endless streaming video options and everything we need ready for delivery, it's all too easy to sit in our homes all the time. It may also seem safer at a time when Covid-19 infection rates are on the increase.

However, staying all the time indoors is not necessarily safer, and the risks of infection are significantly lower during outdoor activities. So, if at all possible, get out for a walk at least several days a week, preferably every day.

5. Procrastination.

When people work from home, their productivity rises, but so do their problems with self-motivation and procrastination. It's simply easier to get down to work when you're in a bustling office surrounded by busy coworkers than when you're at home alone with the TV or games console nearby.

There are several methods to combating procrastination. The most important thing to note is to be gentle with yourself. Keep in mind that procrastination is often the product of anxiety, which we are all experiencing these days.

6. Lack of technical support.

If you're used to calling the IT department whenever anything breaks, you might be in for a world of hurt if your home machine, software, or internet connection fails. If this occurs, you will be able to obtain remote assistance from whoever assisted you at the workplace. You may also be on your own.

The only way to fix this dilemma is to think about it before it happens. What would you do first if your device or internet connection fails? Redundancy is your strongest defense; have a laptop in addition to a desktop, or add a tablet that you can operate on in an emergency. In addition, have a hotspot on your phone or a different computer ready to go in case your internet connection fails.

7. Loneliness.

You may not realize it, but your job is an important part of your social life. In addition, the regular social activities, such as school functions, club meetings, or musical events (which are usually a major part of my life), will be impacted by the pandemic.

It is important to avoid being alone, which is not only bad for your confidence but can also lead to depression and even shorten your life. So, as difficult as it might be these days, prioritize your social life. Meet up with a friend or coworker for a socially distant walk. Or plan a virtual happy hour. (Every Sunday, we have one with some of our friends.)

Even by video chat, socializing is preferable to spending all of your time alone, and it is preferable to rely solely on family or household members for social contact. So make the time and effort to maintain as much social contact as possible. Your productivity, fitness, and even mood will all improve.

Distractions When You Work from Home (And How to Avoid Them!)

There are many benefits to running your own company. You may, for example, set your hours, be your own boss, and work in a more relaxed environment. Working from home often removes the burden of dealing with overbearing, demanding, and demeaning supervisors or colleagues.

However, there are some disadvantages. For example, you are not entitled to paid vacation, holidays, or sick leave. There is no one to back you up or work certain hours for you if you do not work. When you return, the job will still be there.

These are not the only drawbacks. There are also tax implications to think about, as well as the ramifications on your personal life.

However, even if you decide that the benefits outweigh the drawbacks, there are always distractions when working from home.

Distractions include:

1. Children and Other Members of the Family
When you work from home, one of the most common distractions is your children or spouse. Even if the children are all enrolled in school full-time, there are likely to be days when special circumstances hold them at home. The same can be said with a partner who works outside the home.

It can be difficult to get some work done while the kids are running around, talking loudly, watching television, or arguing with each other. A spouse can try to come and talk to you about critical issues or trivial matters.

2. Emails
Checking your email is almost certainly an important part of your job. You most likely have a message to answer to in order to keep your company running.

Nonetheless, it is possible to waste more time than necessary reading and to respond to emails.

3. Cell Phones

Cell phones are another major source of distraction while working from home. You can inadvertently pick up your phone to check on a message and become engrossed in browsing social media posts.

You may also be making the mistake of checking your phone too much. Cell phone overuse is a common cause of lost productivity.

4. Noise

Another major source of distraction when working from home is a noisy atmosphere. Your children or husband could be doing something so loud that it disrupts your thoughts.

It may even be noise from your own making, such as a noisy dishwasher or music you're listening to. Whatever the trigger, excessive noise can make concentrating difficult at times.

5. Other Household Responsibilities

Some of the most common distractions when working from home are actually other household tasks that must be completed. If you are not working in a designated office room, you will be able to see the dishes piling up in the sink or the laundry piling up that needs to be folded.

When you're supposed to be busy, it can be difficult to fight the temptation to rest and finish these tasks.

How to Avoid or Overcome Them:

1. Get the Support of Your Family

When your children or partner are at home while you are trying to function, you must enlist the help of your relatives. Discuss with them, providing you with space and time you need to complete your work.

Inform them that it is important for your career and the payment of your bills. Remind them that taking holidays and enjoying all of the nice stuff they have and do cost money.

Create a signal system that informs your family when it is appropriate to interrupt and when it is not. Create placards to display on your closed office door. Green means it's okay to bother you, yellow means you should ask first, and red means you shouldn't come in right now.

2. Maintain Your Concentration

While working from home, it can be challenging to keep focus and prevent distractions. Checking your email, for example, could be an essential part of your job.

Having said that, testing it all the time is detrimental to getting things done. To stop this habit, just check it in the morning, midmorning, lunch, midafternoon, and at the end of the day.

Set a timer if possible so that you only respond to emails for 15 minutes before returning to your daily job.

3. Turn Off Your Cell Phone

The habit of checking your phone is similar to that of checking your inbox. Simply set it aside in a specified location and check it only after you've checked your email. The majority of the time, forget it so you can focus on more critical tasks.

4. Provide a Dedicated Work Area

Set up a dedicated work area to keep noise disturbances to a minimum. If necessary, set up a separate space as a dedicated office. Keeping your machine, printer, filing system, and other required work tools in a permanent location away from noise and interruptions can boost your productivity.

If you don't have a separate office, create a space dedicated solely to your work. Alternatively, invest in noise-canceling headphones.

5. Set Your Schedule

Set a work schedule that you seldom deviate from to overcome one of the other top distractions while working from home. This will allow you to work when you need to and complete other household duties when you need to.

Remember to schedule a few breaks during the day and a daily mealtime away from work. This will help you remain focused when working and maintain your energy levels at their peak.

When you work from home, there are bound to be many distractions. Nonetheless, the benefits will outweigh the drawbacks and be overcome if you focus on them.

WORKING FROM HOME CAN SAVE YOU MONEY

Is it true that working from home saves money? Aside from the money saved by businesses when workers work remotely, there are other financial advantages of working from home.

Working from home adds significant value to your life because it saves you time, money, stress, and other resources. This chapter delves a little more into how and why working from home will save you money.

If you're currently working from home because you have to, rather than because you want to (thanks, pandemic), you may be missing the office right now. Catered lunches and free cappuccinos at the office can stimulate your appetite more than the meals you've been preparing at home.

And, though you're undoubtedly aware that working from home saves you money (no parking fees, for example), have you sat down to calculate how much you're saving? Your overall sum can differ depending on where you live and the decisions you make. However, we've looked at some common areas where working remotely can save you money.

Costs of Commuting

The average commuter spends $2,000 to $5,000 a year on transportation. Traveling by car is more expensive than using public transportation. But, in any case, the cost of getting to and from work quickly adds up.

Gas

According to the Bureau of Labor Statistics, the average household spent $2,109 in 2018 on "gasoline, other oils, and motor oil" (BLS). This is an improvement from $1,968 the previous year (or a 7.2 percent increase).

The average commuter travels between 5 and 13 miles to work, with some people traveling as far as 47 miles. And all that driving necessitates refueling. A great deal. For example, if you drive 10 miles one way to work and work in the office five days a week, you would most likely fill up once a week. If you get 20 miles per gallon and the average price of gas is $2.60 per gallon, you'll spend $624 on gas alone per year.

However, if you work from home even two days a week, you can spend just $374.40 a year, saving you $249.60. Use a commuting cost calculator to find out how much you spend on gas each year.

You'll spend a lot less money on gas as a remote worker. Of course, you would spend nothing. There are always errands to be run and road trips to be made. However, since your commute is as near as your home office, you can save money. And you won't be doing a lot of driving!

Car Maintenance

Owning a car entails more than just filling the gas tank. There is also upkeep. Oil changes, tire rotations, and all the other routine (and unexpected) maintenance activities you perform to keep your vehicle safe cost money.

Although the annual costs of various cars (electric versus pickup truck, for example) vary, car owners in 2017 could expect to spend between $6,354 and $10,054 on maintenance.

However, it is important to remember that these figures are based on an annual mileage of approximately 15,000 miles. As a remote worker, chances are you drive even less than that. The less you drive, the less wear and tear your car suffers. And the less wear and tear there is, the less often you will have to pay for repairs.

Although this does not actually save money (you still need to change the oil regularly), it allows you to spread your expenses out over a longer time. Furthermore, the less you drive your car, the longer it will possibly last, saving you the cost of replacing your vehicle before you're ready.

Car Insurance

You've already seen the auto insurance ads that illustrate how they're currently providing refunds or credits to policyholders. That's wonderful! But did you know that if you work from home all of the time, you will be able to get permanent lower insurance rates?

When you apply for auto insurance, the insurer will ask you how often you drive. When there are more cars on the roads, people want to commute to and from work. More drivers on the road normally mean more injuries. As a result, you'll have to pay a higher insurance premium because the chances of getting into an accident are higher.

However, the amount of time you spend on the road commuting is equally significant. When you sign up for a policy, the organization will usually ask you for your annual mileage as well as your commuting mileage. These are two separate numbers. Your annual mileage is the amount of time you drive your car in a year, regardless of the cause. Your commuting mileage is the amount of time you spend driving to and from work. The greater your driving mileage, the longer you'll be on the road and the more likely you'll be in an accident.

If you travel less than 5,000 miles for work per year, you might be eligible for a lower insurance premium. The overall annual mileage will determine this, but not driving to work will help reduce your mileage, which could result in a lower insurance premium for you.

Public Transportation

You probably think that public transit is the way to go by now (COVID-19 notwithstanding). Don't be so certain.

First and foremost, not every city has accessible and dependable public transportation. Even when public transit is open, it is not always a viable choice due to schedules or venue.

You have choices in a big metropolitan area. You'll also need a large sum of money.

People who depended solely on public transportation spent between 3% and 4% of their average annual income on public transportation costs in 2017 (the most recent year for which data is available). A commuter in Philadelphia, for example, could pay $96 for a monthly pass or $1,152 per year. Passes in New York City will cost $127 a month or $1,524 a year.

Although considerably less costly than driving, public transportation is still an expense. Working from home is far less expensive than all other modes of transportation.

Clothes

Working in an office, even one with a relaxed dress code, necessitates the wearing of "work" attire. This may include suits, ties, "business casual" clothing, or other formal attire. In 2018, the average household spent $1,866 per year on "apparel and services," which included purchasing and maintaining clothes.

That's right. Your clothes will get dirty no matter what, and you will need to clean them. And, since not everything can be washed, you must factor in dry cleaning costs as well.

Each time you brought your products in for dry-cleaning in 2017, you might expect to pay the following average amounts:

- Two-piece suit: $10 to $15
- Pants: $5 to $8
- Shirt: $5 to $7
- Ties: $3 to $6

However, depending on your industry, you might not be required to wear a suit once a month or even once a week. You might have to put on a suit every day! That dry cleaning can really add up over time.

When you work from home, you do need to buy and clean your clothes, but you certainly don't need a wardrobe full of suits and khakis. Yoga boots, jeans, and a casual tee are typically appropriate. Even better, you don't usually have to dry clean this type of clothes. Tossing them in the washer on laundry day is normally sufficient.

Eating Out

You're probably aware that going out for lunch and buying coffee regularly will quickly add up. This is a purely optional expense that can add up to hundreds of dollars over a year. According to the BLS, the average household spent $3,459 on "food away from home" in 2018.

Even if your workplace offers the best coffee in the world and regular free lunch, don't underestimate the effect commuting can have on your ability to cook. Many a tired commuter has stopped on the way home to pick up pizza because the idea of preparing a meal at the end of the day is just too much.

Eating at home is typically both healthier and less expensive. When you work from home, you can consume whatever foods you want, skip those you don't, and eat whenever you want. And, with a coffee maker, you can make your own java any way you want!

Tax Breaks

If you are a freelancer or self-employed person, you might be eligible for certain tax cuts. If you are a full-time employee who works remotely (either all or some of the time), you might be eligible for tax breaks, but not exactly in the same way as a freelancer might.

- Home office deduction
- Healthcare expenses
- Pass-through deduction
- Retirement contributions
- Depreciation of equipment

Taxes are tricky! However, we have some tax tips that can help you navigate the numerous tax breaks available to remote employees. And, as always, if in doubt, seek the advice of a trained professional.

The Environment

This technically does not save you any money. However, it contributes to preserving the world, which is worth much more than extra cash in your wallet.

According to a 2018 report, almost 3 million tons of greenhouse gases were not emitted into the atmosphere as a result of people working remotely at the time (nearly 3.9 million people). "Rea" Salary

Have you ever tried to put a monetary value on the time you save not commuting and what it means for your financial bottom line? Consider commuting time as part of your overall workday. After all, the whole point of commuting to and from the workplace is to get the work done.

In 2019, the average worker commuted for 27.1 minutes one way, or 54.2 minutes round trip. On the other hand, working from home allows the average former commuter to spend up to 235 fewer hours a year on work-related activities, or around 29 fewer eight-hour days a year. That's almost a month off from work!

So, how does that translate into a raise in your pay? Assume you make $50,000 a year and commute to work. That works out to around $21.70 per hour (because you work an eight-hour day plus your 54-minute commute, for a total of just under nine hours a day). However, if you avoid the commute, your hourly pay will increase to $24.04 per hour!

Time

We're not the first to say it, but time is money. Many people say that time equals satisfaction, and happiness equals work-life balance when working from home.

Working from home saves money because it saves time – time spent waiting in line for the elevator at work, time spent searching for parking so you can catch the train, time spent shopping for work clothing, and time spent commuting by bus.

One of our favorite overall advantages of working remotely is having more time in the day to pursue hobbies. Among these may be time spent on keeping fit, eating well, reading with your children, or working on your burgeoning side hustle – all of which are some of the most forward-thinking job trends open to us right now.

It's difficult to place a monetary value on your time, but according to these figures, the number of hours you save working from home instead of in an office adds up quickly. Though work-at-home jobs aren't for everybody, working from home one to two days a week can really help your bottom line.

Tips to Better Manage Our Money

We just found out how you can save a lot of money by working from home. Now, let's see how to manage this money efficiently so as to maximize the value of our savings.

Being good with money entails more than just getting by. Don't be concerned if you're not a math whiz; great math skills aren't required; you just need to know basic addition and subtraction.

When you have good financial skills, life is much simpler. Your credit score and the amount of debt you end up carrying are affected by how you invest your money. If you're having trouble with money management problems, such as living paycheck to paycheck while earning more than enough money, here are some suggestions to help you change your financial habits.

When faced with a spending decision, particularly one that involves a large purchase, don't just assume you can afford it. Confirm that you can afford it and that you haven't already used those funds for another purpose.

This entails determining whether you can afford a purchase based on your budget and the balances in your checking and savings accounts. Remember that only because the funds are available does not imply that you will make the purchase. You must also remember the bills and expenditures that must be paid before the next payday.

How To Manage Your Money Better

#1 - Have a Budget
Many people do not budget because they do not want to go through what they perceive to be a tedious process of listing expenditures, adding up figures, and ensuring that all is in order. If you're bad with money, there's no place for excuses when it comes to budgeting. Why wouldn't you do it if all it takes to keep your expenses under control is a few hours per month spent working on a budget? Instead of dwelling on the task of making a budget, consider the benefits of budgeting in your life.

#2 - Using the Budget
Your budget is pointless if you make it, then let keep it in a folder on your bookshelf or file cabinet to gather dust. Refer

to it often during the month to help you make spending decisions. It should be updated when you pay bills and spend money on other monthly expenses. You should have an idea of how much money you have available to spend at any given time during the month, taking into account any debts you still owe.

#3 - *Give Yourself a Limit for Unbudgeted Spending*

The net gain, or the amount of money left over after deducting your expenses from your income, is an important component of your budget. If you have some extra money, you can spend it on fun and entertainment, but only up to a certain limit. You can't go crazy with this money, particularly since it isn't much and must last the entire month. Before making any major purchases, be certain that they will not conflict with anything else you have planned.

#4 - *Track Your Spending*

Small expenses add up easily, and before you know it, you've gone through your budget. Begin monitoring your spending to identify areas where you may be unknowingly overspending. Keep your receipts and record your expenses in a spending log, categorizing them so you can find places where you struggle to keep your spending under control.

#5 - *Don't Commit to Any New Recurring Monthly Bills*

Simply because your income and credit qualify you for a loan do not mean you should accept it. Many people mistakenly believe that the bank would not allow them for a credit card or loan that they cannot afford. The bank is only aware of your declared income and the debt obligations on your credit report, not any other obligations that might preclude you from making your payments on time. You have to determine whether a monthly payment is affordable based on your income and other monthly commitments.

#6 - Make Sure You're Paying the Best Prices

You will save money by comparison shopping and ensuring that you are paying the lowest price for goods and services. Look for discounts, coupons, and less expensive alternatives wherever possible.

#7 - Save Up for Big Purchases

The willingness to postpone gratification can go a long way in helping you manage your money better. When you postpone big transactions, rather than sacrificing more critical necessities or placing the transaction on a credit card, you allow yourself more time to consider whether the purchase is worthwhile and even more time to compare costs. You stop paying interest on the transaction if you save instead of using credit. And if you save instead of ignoring payments or commitments, you won't have to live with the many repercussions of failing to pay those bills.

#8 - Limit Your Credit Card Purchases

Credit cards are the worst enemy of a poor spender. When you run out of cash, you immediately reach for your credit cards, regardless of whether you can afford to pay the balance. Resist the temptation to use your credit card to make unaffordable purchases, particularly on things you don't really need.

#9 - Contribute to Savings Regularly
Saving money in a savings account **every month** will help you develop good financial habits. You can also set it up so that money is moved directly from your checking account to your savings account. You won't have to recall to make the transition this way.

#10 - Being Good With Money Takes Practice
You can not be used to planning ahead of time and deferring purchases until you can afford them at first. The more you incorporate these practices into your everyday routine, the simpler it will be to handle your money and the better off your finances will be.

WORK FROM HOME HACKS

I've been working from home for the past ten years, and it's been fascinating to observe the transition in 2020 between in-office and at-home workplaces. According to a PwC study, 55 percent of employees believe that working from home would be a long-term arrangement.

I've had plenty of time to refine a productivity plan that works for me thanks to my long-term work-at-home setup, complete with three kids and a busy household. I've found that it's more than possible to develop a thriving career if you take the time to plan to work from home and establish an environment conducive to professionalism and efficiency.

Tips for Working From Home to Increase Productivity

Staying focused in a workplace with children, immediate access to social media, and an endless number of other distractions can be difficult. Here's how to avoid disruptions and increase efficiency when working from home.

1. Create a Dedicated Office Space

It's all too easy in a busy household to let kids pile their homework on your desk or play on your phone, but this hardly provides a professional environment. You're one of the lucky ones if your house is large enough to contain an entire space devoted solely to work. If not, simply designate a space where you can use your computer, speak on the phone, and store important documents.

Whatever approach you take, it is important to keep your work and personal lives apart. Unless you have no other place to live, keep your bedroom and office separate so that your bed doesn't tempt you during the day or by your laptop at night.

Even if you live alone at home, having a dedicated home office space makes sense — not just to help you stay focused but also to save money on taxes. To qualify for the home office tax deduction, weigh your dedicated office space and determine the percentage of your home it represents — for example, a 200-square-foot office in a 2,000-square-foot home will be 10%. You can then subtract the percentage of your home's expenses, such as electricity and home improvements.

However, in order to apply for the home office deduction, you must use your office solely and daily for business. It no longer qualifies if you just use it occasionally or share it with your whole family. If you have any concerns, contact a tax professional specializing in small-business taxation, such as H&R Block.

2. *Invest in Your Office Inventory*

Your home workspace must have all of the amenities you'd find in a professional office. Of course, what each person considers appropriate varies according to taste and profession. Some things to think about are:

- a dependable, dedicated machine
- a high-quality Internet link
- A landline business phone or a business-only cellphone (look into Xfinity Mobile)
- A file system
- General office supplies (get the best discounts at back-to-school sales)
- A decent printer
- Comfy home office furniture, such as an office chair

Fiddling with an out-of-date machine or dash to the print shop will waste time and productivity. Furthermore, if you are self-employed, you can subtract any things purchased for your home office from your taxes for that year. Just remember to save your receipts.

Take regular inventory and ensure you have everything you need before you begin. That way, you won't have to interrupt your workflow to look for a laptop charger or printer paper.

3. Prioritize Your Day

Setting goals is important at work and much more so when working from home. Without a supervisor looking over your shoulder or coworkers to bounce ideas off of, it's up to you to organize your to-do list. It will assist you in staying on track and avoiding feeling frustrated.

Make a list of all that needs to be accomplished during a given workday, then number each item in order of priority. When the day is over, pass everything you didn't get done to the next day's list right away to ensure that nothing falls through the cracks.

Apps and software will also help you stay on track. TeuxDeux is a great app for making and prioritizing lists, as well as taking notes online. If you'd rather handle your to-do list on your mobile, try to Remember the Milk, which works with Alexa, Google Assistant, and Siri to let you make lists by voice rather than typing them. Do it Tomorrow, which is available for iOS and Android, is another option. It is beneficial to plan your to-do list a day ahead of time so that nothing falls through the cracks — even though you are unable to complete it today.

4. Get Your Family Involved

If you work from home with children, you will need everyone's cooperation. Call a family meeting and inform your children that you must concentrate during work hours. Discuss your schedule with your partner and trade-off child care responsibilities if you both work from home so that you each have dedicated time to concentrate.

One family I know employs a "stoplight scheme." Based on the day's events, the work-at-home parent paints a red, yellow, or green circle on the office door. Green means enter immediately, yellow means inquire first, and red means do not interrupt. It turns efficiency into a game for kids in a visual and easy-to-understand format.

Even if you don't have children, you may need to express your desire for a quiet working atmosphere to your partner. If your spouse or partner works in a more conventional environment, the concept of a home office can seem casual to them, resulting in noise and distractions while you're trying to focus. Establish ground rules for your workplace, such as knocking before entering your office or keeping quiet between certain hours.

5. Stay on Task

When you're telecommuting, it's essential to check your email, particularly if it's your coworkers' preferred method of communication. On the other hand, constantly clicking on the email tab will stymie your own projects and interrupt workflow.

Close your account, turn off all phone alerts, and check your texts and social media only at set times during the day. Even if you check every 30 minutes, you'll get some nice, uninterrupted work time.

Another choice for keeping a clean inbox and avoiding distractions from personal messages is to create a separate email address for work and make an effort to read, sort, and reply to correspondence accordingly.

If you have a habit of visiting your favorite websites while you should be working, try LeechBlock, an extension that allows you to "ban" time-wasting websites between certain hours. You can also schedule "allowed" check-in times, such as five minutes on Facebook after 45 minutes of work.

6. Use a Dedicated Browser

On my computer, I have two browsers: one for work and one for casual browsing. Open tabs, bookmarks, email messages, and messaging are all distractions in the casual surfing browser. When I have free time, I use my web browser to quickly search my favorite websites and communicate with others.

My work browser, on the other hand, is nearly empty. I just save job-related bookmarks and use applications and extensions to help me remain efficient. As a result, you can use the Internet without being interrupted by funny videos or social networking feeds.

7. Get Organized

When you work from home, your job can become even more difficult. You're suddenly juggling home and work life, and a crammed schedule can interrupt your workflow. That means you must optimize and arrange your home office to the best of your ability.

Getting prepared before you sit down at your desk will help you be less depressed and more efficient during the day. Evernote is one of my favorite apps for keeping organized. It helps you to keep thoughts, notes, photos, and reminders all in one place, making it ideal for that "eureka" moment when you're not at your desk.

Keeping your office tidy will also help you keep on top of things. You will spend less time looking for loose papers if you organize and file them. A filing cabinet costs about $50 and more than pays for itself in terms of time saved and improved productivity. It also improves the quality of your working environment.

8. Set Office Hours

When your screen is just a few feet away, it can be difficult to distinguish between your personal and professional lives. Creating a daily schedule is the most effective way to promote work-life balance. Although it may be impractical to fully disregard your work after hours, particularly if you work as a freelancer with strict deadlines, you can always prioritize. Set a rule that your work hours are from 9 a.m. to 5 p.m., and you only respond to urgent emails after that.

If your work allows you to monitor your hours, an app like Toggl can be extremely useful. It keeps track of how much time you worked and helps you to give reminders and timesheets to your bosses. Even if you don't have to turn in your hours, it will help you be more productive by telling you how long you worked on a project and how much time you spent browsing the Web.

Just keep in mind that *you can also account for breaks and meals when preparing your work schedule*. They're an essential part of keeping your sanity. A morning break, a midday lunch, and an afternoon break — even if it's just to relax and browse your favorite websites — will help you stay focused and stop getting sidetracked while you should be working.

9. Eat in the Kitchen

When you work from home, eating at your desk will seem like a no-brainer, but I find that if I keep a snack at my computer, the act of eating quickly distracts me. Since it's almost impossible for me to function when one hand delivers food to my mouth, I typically use it as an excuse to take a break and browse the Web instead.

Making your home office a no-food zone is your best bet. Keep a water bottle or a cup of coffee nearby for easy sips, but leave the main meal to the kitchen or dining room. You get a well-deserved break, but when you return to your desk, you're ready to get back to work. Remember to quickly clean up after eating, so you aren't distracted by a sink full of dishes.

10. Invest in Headphones

If you're easily distracted, a decent pair of noise-canceling headphones might be one of the best investments you ever make. Consider all of the sounds in your home that can interfere with your concentration. A ringing phone, a noisy television, children playing, the doorbell, and even normal conversations can cause you to lose your train of thinking or become irritated. And, because it's not realistic (or fair) to expect all noise to stop while you're working, noise-canceling headphones are the next best thing.

Noise-canceling headphones emit a frequency that helps muffle common household noises, and they work particularly well when combined with music. Similarly, the White Noise Lite software for iOS or Android can be extremely useful. When you're in the region, simply turn on some ocean sounds to help you concentrate on your job.

Headphones are also a perfect sign for your family — if they are on, it means you are working and should not be bothered.

11. Use Cloud-Based File Sharing

Telecommuting will entail constantly exchanging files between your home and the offices of your business or clients. While emailing back and forth is possible, file attachments may get lost in the shuffle, particularly if you're frequently updating copies.

A cloud-based file-sharing service, such as Dropbox, Google Drive, or Trello, is an ideal solution. File sharing, with its ability to update in real-time, almost entirely removes the issue of dealing with out-of-date papers. You may also bypass previous files to avoid confusion, granting access to friends, bosses, or clients. It also holds large files that take up a lot of space out of your inbox.

12. Keep an Impeccable Calendar

Being at home all day will entail a lot of multitasking, such as driving kids to appointments or talking on the phone during your lunch break. A well-maintained calendar will assist you in avoiding overscheduling and double-booking. Use whatever works best for you, whether it's a paper diary, your phone's schedule, or an app to help you stay organized.

Furthermore, attempting to communicate with colleagues and customers while you are not in the same physical workplace can be difficult. Set up meetings on a community Google calendar so that everyone can check-in and select a time slot that works for them. You may also submit invites and confirmations, which will be added to the calendar as appropriate.

13. Ask for Help

You don't have to do it all by yourself. Hire a babysitter for your children via Care.com, or consider hiring a virtual assistant or housekeeper, or even sharing duties with a neighbor or friend to help minimize the reach of your obligations and allow you to concentrate. If it's in the budget, asking for help alleviates the stress of juggling it. You'll be able to be more efficient if you know your other obligations are being taken care of.

Working from home, whether you have children or are traveling solo, means you are constantly reminded of all the chores you need to do, adding a layer of tension to traditional office work. If you feel like you're falling behind, ask your partner or older children to chip in and take on the tasks that are distracting you the most. You would be more efficient if you concentrate solely on your job and not on the dirty dishes in the sink or the errands you need to run.

Handy.com is a perfect choice if you need to hire cleaners for your house. You'll be able to manage everything online, and you'll be able to schedule them to come as often as you like.

14. Get Out and Socialize

It's all too easy to become virtually glued to your office chair, particularly when it's close to your kitchen and bed — after all, what else do you need? However, if you work from home, you must make an effort to get out of the house and socialize regularly. A weekly Zoom call with your colleagues, for example, will help you feel more connected.

If you are too busy to get out of the house and engage with others, think of it as part of your work and schedule time away from your desk as an appointment. Even if it's just going to the park for some fresh air and a wave to your friends, taking a break, getting outside, and talking to people during the day would make you feel a lot more human.

15. *Tap Into Your Ultradian Cycle*

You've already heard of the circadian cycle, which controls your sleep and wake cycles. However, the lesser-known ultradian cycle, which governs your rest and activity cycles, may be the secret to unlocking efficiency. Essentially, most people's brains can handle peak productivity for around 90 minutes before needing a 20-minute break for a less demanding mission. This pattern represents your ultradian period.

Pushing yourself to be hyper-productive without allowing your brain any rest leads to burnout because humans aren't designed to concentrate for long periods at a time. It's the same concept as the Pomodoro Technique, which employs 25-minute work blocks separated by five-minute breaks.

Everyone is different, so try checking your concentration by setting a timer and seeing how long you can focus on a task before becoming fatigued. Then, you can make the most of those blocks of time by incorporating "brain rests" during the day. You can walk your dog, browse through social media, make a snack, or read the news knowing that when you're finished, you'll be more concentrated and efficient.

Soft Skills Remote Workers Need

Soft skills are not as gentle as they seem. In reality, they can make or break your career, particularly if you work from home.

Soft skills—defined as "general characteristics that help workers succeed in the workplace, regardless of their seniority level, position, or industry"—have come to the forefront in hiring and recruiting decisions as the professional world settles into a new standard of working from home.

There are more remote jobs available than ever before, but there are still more remote job seekers. With a low unemployment rate and the regional versatility of remote work, the market is flooded with applicants, all of whom are technically equal. Hard skills are essential in a crowded recruiting pool, but soft skills will help you rise to the top.

FlexJobs and PAIRIN recently compiled a list of the top ten remote-work fields between March 1 and November 30 of last year, as well as the top five soft skills for each region. If you're trying to break into a new area or advance in your current one, knowing which social and interpersonal skills will better complement your technological abilities in the workplace is beneficial.

Here are the top 25 soft skills and characteristics for success in remote work, as described by the FlexJobs-PAIRIN study.

Accountability means "being answerable." To accept accountability for results through sufficient resource usage, personal honesty, and self-monitoring" This skill is particularly valuable in the field of Medical & Health remote work.

Assertiveness is described as"global proclivity to express and communicate with boldness, enthusiasm, and confidence" Remote staff in Sales, Customer Service, and Marketing must be assertive.

Collaboration and teamwork are described as "combining efforts and resources with others toward a common goal." To collaborate with diverse teams efficiently and respectfully," Candidates for remote positions in Project Management should emphasize this ability.

Compliance is described as"global tendencies to maintain self-control and adhere to another's strategy, rules, will, or direction" This ability is especially important for remote work in the Medical & Health and Accounting & Finance industries.

Conflict resolution is described as "the ability to effectively negotiate and resolve disagreements." Being able to effectively resolve disagreements is essential in all fields, but particularly in Sales, Accounting & Finance, and Customer Service.

Cooperative-Practical: "The moderation of reason and emotion, resulting in calm, commonsense thinking — upbeat, sensitive, and realistic" This personality trait is in high demand in the fields of Education & Training and Business Development remote work.

Creativity is described as "the ability to think, do, and express oneself in ways that differ from the norm." Personal elaborations or variants on proven or current techniques are included" This characteristic should be shown by professionals working from home in the Computer & IT and Education & Training fields.

Critical thinking is described as "gathering and critically evaluating key information as a guide to belief or action." Analysis, conceptualization, synthesis, and assessment are all part of the intellectual process" Computer & IT, Accounting & Finance, and Business Development are all remote-work areas that require this expertise.

Dynamism is described as "global tendencies to produce results through deliberate, resourceful, and energetic mindsets and behaviors." This characteristic is important for Project Management professionals who work remotely.

Enriching Others is described as "perceiving and reacting to others with acceptance and respect while promoting their growth to full potential." When they work remotely, business development practitioners, in particular, can maintain this mindset.

Flamboyance is described as "the desire to impress or excite — to arouse others through words or acts." Flamboyance is a desirable characteristic in the Marketing and Administrative fields, and the ability to communicate it remotely is even more important.

Influential leadership is described as "the ability to positively influence the choices of others by concentrating on what is essential to them and building consensus." By concentrating on this talent, sales and marketing professionals will advance their remote careers.

Inspirational leadership is described as "the ability to uplift, enliven, fill, and inspire others through a compelling vision." Marketing professionals, in particular, can cultivate this ability in their remote work relationships.

Objective-Analytical: "The priority of rationality and fact-based evaluating over emotions, resulting in consistency, thoroughness, and productivity" This ability is needed in the computer and information technology fields.

Originality is described as "the ability to create or independently conceive of completely new concepts, processes, or items, regardless of their utility" The ability to think creatively is essential in the fields of computer science and information technology, as well as education and training, particularly in light of the numerous new challenges posed by remote work.

Perspective is described as "the capacity to comprehend widely, to organize information and experience, and to provide clear-sighted and practical advice to others." A facet of wisdom" This is yet another trait that is beneficial in all fields, especially education and training.

Problem Solving is described as "discovering, analyzing, and solving a variety of unfamiliar problems in both traditional and innovative ways." Computer and information technology experts who work remotely should have good problem-solving skills.

Productivity is described as "the ability to set and achieve targets in the face of challenges and competing pressures." To prioritize, schedule, and execute work in order to achieve the desired outcomes" Productive Project Management practitioners may increase the value of their remote work.

Relationship Management: "The ability to handle relationships effectively by becoming mindful of one's own feelings as well as those of others" This interpersonal ability is particularly important in the Project Management field in the age of remote work.

Relationship: "the desire to be close to and loyal to another individual or people — to genuinely bond with and enjoyably associate with them" This soft skill is useful for remote work in a variety of fields, including accounting and finance, marketing, business development, and administration.

Self Assessment: "To engage in self-reflection in order to assess one's beliefs, skills, and resources' strengths and limitations" This skill is especially important for Business Development professionals.

Service Orientation: "The ability to predict, recognize, and fulfill people's sometimes unspoken needs through assistance, goods, or services, as well as the desire to generate customer satisfaction and loyalty" This is another essential skill for a variety of industries transitioning to a remote workforce, including Medical & Health, Sales, Customer Service, and Administrative.

Social awareness is described as "the ability to relate to and react to the feelings, needs, and concerns of individuals or larger societal groups" Professionals in a variety of fields, including Medical & Health, Sales, Accounting & Finance, and Education & Training, will benefit from developing this expertise.

Stress Tolerance is described as "the ability to withstand pressure and uncertainty without being negative (e.g., hopeless, angry, or hostile) against oneself or others." Stress tolerance is essential for all remote workers, particularly those in fast-paced fields such as Customer Service, Administrative, and Project Management.

Supportiveness is described as "the desire to help, protect, and care for those who are in emotional or physical need" This empathetic trait will help medical and health practitioners, customer service representatives, and administrative professionals advance in their remote-work careers.

3 Steps to Cultivate Soft Skills

Did any skills stand out to you as areas for growth as you read through the list? Perhaps you are already aware of the areas in which you should improve. So, where do you begin?

Determine the soft skills you already have.

Starting with a constructive appraisal will inspire you to continue developing and empowering you to acquire more soft skills. Some online services offer soft skills testing so people can identify their areas of strength and where they can improve. I often suggest conducting a self-audit to assess the soft skills you are most confident in and which you are least confident in. Inquiring with people close to you, such as friends, relatives, and colleagues, will also provide insight into where you can go from here.

Take a class.

There are several free, online short and long courses available to help you improve your skills (for example, see https://esoftskills.com/soft-skills-training). And, after you've completed a course, it's time to practice — at work and in your personal life. You may also look for new activities or projects at work, volunteering, in your neighborhood, or at home where you can apply your newer skills.

Interview anyone who possesses the desired abilities.

Informational interviews are also an excellent way to learn from those already proficient in the skills you wish to develop. For example, if your sister-in-law has excellent stress tolerance and you've observed her remaining calm in stressful circumstances, ask her how she handles stress and what advice she has for you to improve in this field.

Everything boils down to communication.

Critical Thinking, Service Orientation, Social Awareness, Relationship Management, and Stress Tolerance are the top soft skills in most sectors, in my opinion. Surprisingly, all of these abilities are built on the ability to communicate effectively. Communication is the most sought-after skill by employers of remote teams.

What is the significance of contact in the virtual workplace? Positive rapport is critical to team success, but it can be difficult to establish behind a computer. Most remote employers tend to recruit professionals who can both do the job and establish strong working relationships with their coworkers.

The bottom line is that employers trust people with strong interpersonal and communication skills.

Many applicants would have similar technological competencies in today's highly competitive remote job market. These not-so-soft skills are what will set you apart — and place you in the best position to get the job.

SETTING UP YOUR HOME WORKSPACE

A home office can be everything you want it to be, and it can be wherever you want it to be. The choices are only restricted by your room and imagination, whether in a cozy corner or spread out around the basement.

We know from data that workspace design is essential, but how do you apply that to your work from the home environment? In this unprecedented age, when people are often indoors and separated from one another, it is critical to understand the importance of curating and designing your personal workspace at home. Working remotely provides a one-of-a-kind opportunity to create a new space for efficiency, innovation, and connection. Although preserving work/life balance in this new world is not as easy as reading the words in this post, these suggestions are intended to provide small ways to enhance your mental health, efficiency, and maybe even your interior-decorating game.

Here are some tips for choosing the most efficient WFH place, properly lighting it, and finding a desk and chair combination that will keep you comfortable in the coming weeks. Keep these suggestions in mind as you try to build a better workspace.

How to Set Up a Home Office

Working from home has many benefits, not the least of which is a 30-second commute. And, while many people believe that working from home entails working on the sofa, in the garden, or even from your bed, you may discover that you are most effective at home when you work at a "proper" workstation. You know, the kind with a chair and a desk.

When you set up your home office, you have a lot of options and freedom. Do you want a chair that is purple and orange? Take a chance! Do you want striped walls? Please accept our invitation! However, regardless of how you decorate, furnish, or set up your home office, we have some pointers to help you build a room that contributes to your work-from-home success.

Find the Best Location

Choosing a location for a home office is simple for certain people. They have a spare room that they use as a dedicated office space. While it may be an actual "office," many people prefer an empty bedroom or even the basement. However, not everyone has so much empty room in their house. As the room is limited, you must be imaginative with your "office space."

If you don't mind packing up your office before every meal, you can still use a portion of the kitchen table as your office room. However, resetting your office after each meal might not be appealing to you. In that case, you can have to consider being imaginative with the room you already have. Examine unused corners in larger spaces, big (but empty) closets, and even the space under the stairs! With a little imagination, several spaces can be converted to an office.

Add Privacy
If you're lucky enough to have a dedicated office space, it's likely to have walls that extend all the way from the floor to the ceiling and sturdy doors that close. As a result, privacy and silence are easy to come by. However, if your office is in, say, the corner of your bedroom, it can be difficult to distinguish work from home.

Consider installing a privacy divider in your home office. Traditional dividers that sit on the floor are accessible. Alternatively, you might hang a curtain from the ceiling or from a rod. Curtains are a lightweight and relatively low-cost way of "closing the door" on your office. With a curtain, you can select something subtle that complements the rest of the decor. Alternatively, pick something wild and insane to energize your "door."

Consider Who Else Uses the Space

Remember who else will use your home office when you set it up, and choose the room and furniture accordingly. Would your children use the office for homework, and will your partner work from home as well? Consider a partner desk arrangement, in which two people will work at the same desk at the same time.

Are there any visitors? You could meet with them in the living room, but that isn't always the best option. Be sure to provide seating and table space for clients as well.

Invest in Yourself

In many ways, investing in a home office system is an investment in yourself. You want to build a professional atmosphere in which you can be both efficient and relaxed. However, as with many investments, you get what you pay for. And, while it might be tempting to buy "cheap" office furniture, keep in mind what that low price gets you.

If you work 40 hours a week in your home office, make sure you consider consistency. If you have to upgrade your desk in a year or two, the cheapest desk will not save you money in the long run.

Prioritize Comfort

When you work from home, it can be tempting to simply take a chair from the dining room. Sitting at a desk for long periods without adequate back support, on the other hand, is a surefire way to develop posture issues. Ergonomic office chairs have the proper comfort when sitting for long time. Like the rest of your home office furniture, purchasing a supportive chair is an investment in yourself.

Brown recommends that home office staff search for the following characteristics in an ergonomic chair:

- Height adjustable
- 360-degree swivel base
- Adjustable backrest and armrest
- Adjustable seat depth
- Built-in lumbar support

Support Your Neck and Eyes

Don't forget to take care of your neck and eyes as well. Ascertain that your monitor is in the "ideal" position. Since that position is unique to each person, you'll have to play with placement. Here are some pointers to help you get it right:

- Keep the spine in a neutral place at all times, and keep the top of the frame at or just below eye level.
- Place the display at least 20 inches away from your eyes or further away if you have a big monitor.

- When looking at the center of the frame, your eyes should be slightly down to help keep your neck in good alignment. Tilt the monitor back 10 to 20 degrees to ensure you're looking down at an angle on the screen. If you wear bifocals, tilt the screen back 30 to 45 degrees to avoid tilting your head back to concentrate.
- The majority of displays can be adjusted. However, often that is insufficient, and you can need to invest in a screen riser to get the proper adjustment. In a pinch, some books or an old box can also suffice.

Get the Right Desk

Working from home entails spending a significant amount of time at your desk. So you want to buy a desk that suits your budget, workflow, and room. You will want a desk that helps you remain productive by keeping you relaxed during the day.

Sitting and standing all day can also cause aches and pains, as well as long-term health problems. Consider having a standing desk instead of a conventional "set" desk, but it can take some getting used to. With an ergonomic height adjustable desk, you can sit when you want and spread your legs when you need to by simply pushing a button to raise your desk to standing height.

Standing desks can be better for you than sitting desks in terms of reducing aches and pains. Let's be honest.

Sedentism pervades modern life. Working at a desk all day (while possibly snacking) isn't good for your well-being. Standing desks tend to be healthier than sitting desks. According to one report, standing six hours a day instead of sitting at a desk for the same amount of time resulted in a 5.5-pound weight loss per year. Although it is not the same as an hour at the gym, using a standing desk can benefit your long-term health.

Stash It Away

When we think of remote work supplies, we always envision a laptop...and not much else. However, you'll almost certainly have some journals, pens, and other office supplies lying around depending on your work. And, yes, there are some paper files to keep track of.

Dedicated storage solutions are beneficial for more than just the rest of your household products. They can also be used to store files, journals, stationery, and other things in your home office. It does not have to be a giant filing cabinet or a massive desk with drawers. A simple cubby system with small bins could suffice. Plastic storage tubs may also be useful if you need to pack up your office at the end of the day. Even if you just clear a small section of an existing shelving unit and devote it to work products, you'll feel more organized right away.

Protect Sensitive or Important Documents

On the other hand, shelves and cubbies are not the only options for all of your storage needs. There are some sensitive documents that you should not leave lying around the office, particularly if it is a shared room. Brown urges people to "invest in lockable file and storage cabinets" when they have things they don't want to lose.

Fortunately, locking cabinets do not have to be made of "ugly neutral colored metal." There are several safe, locking cabinets and drawers that are also attractive and stylish.

Think Up and Down

Yes. A home office has certain disadvantages. One issue is those home offices, even if they are in a dedicated space, are typically small. Don't ever consider side to side while setting up your home office. To optimize your storage options, think vertically as well. A hutch, tall bookcases, or even floating shelves will provide you with additional storage without taking up valuable floor space.

Tame the Wires

Although Wi-Fi is available anywhere, that doesn't mean you won't have a lot of cords in your office. And your mobile devices need charging from time to time. You can still rely on cords, cords, and more cords in your home office.

Consider purchasing a cord control system. This can be as basic as a twist tie or something a little more formal, but whatever you get, make sure you use it. Also, if your office is in a dedicated but public location, consider where the outlets are when you set up shop. You could not have many choices and end up running power strips and extension cords around the floor. If that is the case, make sure you find a discreet way to do it (like with cord covers).

Also, when you're setting up the wires, consider the Wi-Fi. There might be days when you choose to work from home rather than in the workplace. If you plan to work on the couch or even outside on some days, test your router to ensure that the link not only reaches but is also strong. To work on the patio and remain linked, you can need to invest in a Wi-Fi extender or even a Wi-Fi mesh device.

Light It Up

When it comes to setting up a home office, lighting is frequently neglected. Most work is done on machines, so what's the big deal if monitors (and even keyboards) light up?

Quite a bit. Although bad office lighting will not cause blindness, it will cause you to strain your eyes. Eye pressure can cause headaches over time, making you a less efficient employee.

Set up your home office in an area that receives as much natural light as possible. It will make you feel better and may even increase your productivity. Using natural light to light your office is better for the atmosphere, if nothing else.

When natural light is not available, or you simply need more light, invest in the appropriate lamps. If you can believe that overhead lighting is the best option, it may produce a glare on your computer or desk, making it difficult to see. Having said that, a task lamp will also help you shine a light exactly where you need it. Look for a task lamp with a solid shade that can be directed directly at your desk when needed.

However, indirect lighting could be a better option for you. In indirect lighting, lampshades or diffusers soften the light, reducing glare and make it easier on the eyes. Only make sure the light isn't too diffused, or you might lose sight of what you're doing.

Improve Your Internet Connection for Remote Working

With millions of people now using the virtual workplace, you might be wondering how to boost your internet connectivity when working remotely.

Working from home is more than a passing fad, a perks package, or a band-aid solution to the latest COVID-19 pandemic. Many businesses are switching to permanent work-from-home positions, indicating that remote work is here to stay. It has become the new standard for millions of workers in USA and around the world. When workers transition to this modern virtual workplace, it is clear that technological criteria will play a significant role in the success of work-from-home positions.

The most critical thing you need to excel in remote work roles as a work-from-home employee is a secure internet connection. This will allow you to finish your work, interact with colleagues, and communicate with clients and customers. It is possible to have grainy video calls, long loading times, and connectivity problems if you do not have a strong internet signal.

Unfortunately, many remote employees are forced to make do with the few major telecommunications providers and the internet coverage and plans that are available, at least before internet access is classified as a public utility. If you've decided on the best internet package for your needs, there are a few things you can do to ensure that the internet signal in your home workspace is as good as possible.

Get the Right Tools

If you want to increase the speed of your internet connection when operating remotely, as well as the total area covered, several key pieces of technology can assist you.

The WIFI/WLAN Extender: A portable system that links to an existing WIFI network and duplicates the signal. The duplicated signal is then broadcasted, enabling you to switch the Extender to a new position far away from the router, significantly expanding the WIFI range.

The WIFI/WLAN Repeater: This system connects directly to your existing router via an ethernet cable, giving it more power and capability. As a result, both range and maximum transmission speed are significantly increased.

There are numerous boosters, repeaters, and extenders available that will ideally provide you with a stronger WIFI signal, enabling you to operate from any location in your house. Finding the right system for you will be determined by your unique requirements and existing equipment, and some research will assist you in determining what will best fit your room. Don't be afraid to call or email the manufacturer or the store where you purchased your computer, as they should be able to provide a more thorough technical rundown.

Once you've got the right technology, there are a few things you can do to boost your internet connectivity when working remotely.

The Room Matters

Converting your home into a remote workspace can often result in the development of home workspaces in unexpected locations. When you have a family, roommates, and shared living space, your choices can quickly become limited. Bedrooms, basements, and kitchens are typical home workspaces. Still, attics, laundry rooms, balconies, and other unconventional locations may be pressed into operation to meet the needs of workers transitioning to working from home. Where possible, select a location that receives a strong WIFI signal. This can necessitate some experimentation and change, such as relocating your workspace or rearranging the bed.

Set up your router at the proper height.

The height at which you position your router may have a significant effect on your WIFI internet signal. Consider a speaker; speakers that are higher in the air are easier to hear and have better sound quality. The same holds true for your router. Changing the height of your router is an easy way to boost your internet connection when operating remotely.

The ideal height for your router is 1-1.5 meters (3-4 feet) off the ground. This is the optimum height for the WIFI signal to spread. It also has the added benefit of elevating your router, which protects it from harm.

However, don't set it too high, as this will cause your signal to degrade.

Place Your Router in a Central Location

Putting your router in a central position in your home would boost your internet connectivity when operating remotely. Many people position their router in the corner of a room and then forget about it, only to be annoyed by a poor WIFI signal one floor up or down. It is important to locate the router in the center of the workspace. The basement or attic are not ideal for multilevel homes because they raise the distance that the signal must travel to reach you.

Avoid putting your router behind furniture or on the other side of a wall when choosing a central spot. Large pieces of furniture and walls will actually block the router's WIFI signal, resulting in a significant loss of speed and reliability.

Furthermore, such electrical appliances have been known to cause signal interference. If your signal is unstable, consider switching your router away from televisions, refrigerators, microwaves, and other electronic devices to see if the signal quality improves.

What Do You Do If Your Router Breaks Down?

If you have issues with your router, contact your internet service provider right away. They might experience a power outage or give you detailed instructions about how to reset your router. Inform the bosses and colleagues as soon as possible if there is a prolonged outage. A communication breakdown is not only bad for efficiency, but it can also affect positive organizational culture and workplace environment. Dealing with a poor internet connection is aggravating, but your coworkers will be much more irritated if they have no notice that work will be postponed or that you will be unable to respond to their inquiries.

Unplugging your router and any wired WIFI extender or repeater is an easy solution if you want to find a fast fix before calling your internet provider. Wait at least 10 seconds before plugging in your computers again. After a few moments, the router can re-emit a signal. Check to see if you can bind, and you should be good to go.

Working from home needs a reliable internet connection. Although there is only so much we can do with the small number of internet providers, finding ways to enhance your internet access while working remotely should be on everyone's work-from-home to-do list once you've chosen a provider. This will allow you to keep in touch with colleagues and do your job to the best of your abilities.

Remote Work Apps For Every Work-From-Home Professional

Working from home isn't always easy. Some people struggle to remain active in their home office, while others struggle to communicate with their customers or team members.

Fortunately, many remote work applications are available today that will help you keep track of your tasks and make your online job easier. After all, you don't need to complicate your life any further than necessary.

Here's a list of amazing tools to improve your work-from-home performance immediately!

1. Communication

Communication is one of the most critical and one of the most difficult aspects of working remotely. Being apart from your teammates or customers in the same office can be a serious problem. The remote work tools mentioned below will assist you in staying linked as effectively as possible.

Google Hangouts

Looking for a Skype substitute? Google Hangouts is a fantastic and reliable choice for audio and video meetings. If you use Slack, it is simple to implement and will ease your working life.

HipChat

HipChat is another messaging application that is gaining popularity. It is particularly useful if you use Jira or some other Atlassian product because it suits the definition perfectly.

Jing

It can be difficult to describe a job to a coworker who is not right next to you. Jing is a lightweight solution for creating screencasts of up to five minutes in length. Then you can upload it and get a shareable connection. Emails or screenshots are less time-consuming and confusing.

Join.me

Join.me not only allows you to make audio and video calls with your team, but it also allows you to share your screen with others. Ideal for last-minute meetings.

Slack

Slack is one of the most widely used remote work applications. People who use it are more likely to refer to it as a religion than anything else. You can communicate with your team members in real time thanks to the real-time chat. You'll also find amusing gifs, helpful chatbots, and a plethora of integrations to help you cut down on email.

Zoom

Zoom will be your first choice if you work in very large teams and need a meeting tool that allows you to host a large number of people. Meetings may also be recorded and broadcast for future reference.

2. Team Feedback

When managing a remote team, having great communication resources isn't always enough. Here are the best tools for you if you need instant feedback or want to gauge the current team's mood.

Chimp or Champ

While Chimp or Champ is not an app, it can be extremely useful for managing remote teams. Consider a feedback box on the internet. It enables the team to provide useful input and easily assess their level of satisfaction.

Doodle

Want to find the best time for the next team meeting or get feedback on a new decision? Doodle is an excellent tool for sending out short polls of any kind and receiving fast responses.

OfficeVibe

OfficeVibe is an excellent tool for tracking employee satisfaction and happiness. Team members receive direct messages daily with questions to answer their overall mood, feelings toward the team, etc. The responses are then secretly sent to the team leader (or whoever you put in charge).

3. File Management

File management is a critical component when operating remotely. When you collaborate with others, you must find a way to store the data to see, edit, and build it. Fortunately, there are many solutions to this issue.

Box

Box is a perfect alternative to Google Drive and Dropbox for safely storing and sharing essential files. It is also simple to integrate with tools such as Office 365, Google Apps, and Slack.

Dropbox

Dropbox is a well-known cloud storage service that is free to use but has restricted storage space. Save your files and, if necessary, share them with others, allowing them to edit or add new material.

Google Drive

Collaborative work from a distance can seem difficult, but Google Drive makes it easy. It is a multi-purpose platform that allows you to store and exchange files as well as interact in collaborative online word processors, spreadsheets, and presentation slides.

In Google Docs, you will create project plans, write and update blog posts, and create business documents. In Google

Sheets (where you can also generate accompanying charts and graphs), you will be able to compile and manipulate statistical data for your business. Google Slides allows you to create (and later present) presentations for clients and teammates.

You can easily generate any of the types of documents mentioned above in Google Drive and then collaborate on them in real-time. All of your updates and edits will be synced and saved automatically. Aside from that, you'll be able to drag and drop video, audio, and text files (up to 10Gb per file) and then share access to them with teammates.

When you use Google Drive for Android, you can take pictures of documents you want to save (such as receipts or statements) directly from the app, and they will be saved as PDFs in the drive.

Quip
Quip is a file-sharing service similar to Google Docs. It enables teams to collaborate by allowing them to discuss documents, spreadsheets, and task lists. You can leave feedback, approve or deny versions.

4. *Time Tracking*

When you work as a freelancer, you need a way to monitor your time so that you can better bill your clients. However, even though you are working, your employer will need proof of what you are doing and how long it takes you.

As a result, one of the following tools should be included in any remote worker's starter kit.

Time Doctor

So far, Time Doctor is my favorite time tracking app. It allows you to keep track of the projects you're working on and also reminds you to stay focused if you get distracted by items like Facebook or YouTube. It creates bills for your clients automatically and integrates with several common project management tools. This is a fantastic way to remain active!

Hours

Hours is an easy and straightforward method for logging all of your hours in one location. It provides a visual timeline as well as reminders and reports. That is everything there is to it. There are no extraneous features to distract you. Concentrate solely on your hours.

Toggl

Toggl is another major player in the time tracking market. You are provided with a convenient dashboard from which to review and generate reports. Furthermore, you can integrate it with other apps such as Todoist or Asana.

Teamweek

Teamweek allows you to visually schedule your time. The events can then be viewed by the entire team in an open calendar. It has an amazing interface and is easy to use.

Harvest

Harvest allows you to monitor your team's progress and generate updates for projects, team members, and customers. You can also record expenses, review payment capacities, see the company's profitability, and request timesheet approvals.

Hubstaff

Need a little push to get the job done? Hubstaff takes occasional screenshots of what you're doing (it's too dangerous to spend all day on Facebook) and helps you to generate reliable time reports.

5. Project Management

A project management app is critical for dispersed teams, but it can also be useful for many freelancers or entrepreneurs who collaborate with clients or business partners.

There are numerous project management applications available. You must test and evaluate the tasks that your team requires and the user interface that you prefer.

Asana

Asana is very popular amongst bigger businesses. It is a professional and powerful project management app with impressive layouts to organize projects between many team members.

Trello

If you've only heard of one project management app in your entire life, chances are it's Trello. Using various boards, this versatile method lets you arrange to-dos and tasks. It's also ideal for sharing with team members.

Basecamp

Suppose you are a freelancer looking for smart project management software. In that case, Basecamp is a platform that allows you to manage your staff, programs, and tasks while still collaborating directly with clients.

Though Asana is perfect for team coordination and monitoring project progress, Basecamp is ideal for involving clients directly in the project and consulting with them while working. You'll be able to exchange to-dos with clients, message them, and forward client emails directly to Basecamp — all while keeping it special for the team and hidden from clients.

You will also be able to build to-do lists, interact in message boards, monitor deadlines in calendar schedules, store files and documents, engage in real-time group chats, and do everything else required to streamline project communication within a team. You'll be able to regularly ask your team check-in questions (such as "What did you work on today?") and have all responses rolled up in one easily searchable thread.

Float

Float is an excellent choice for smaller teams because it allows you to manage resources and monitor projects. It is easy to customize and use.

JIRA

JIRA is yet another excellent choice for project management and problem monitoring. It's a pretty stable app that's ideal for handling job sprints.

MeisterTask

MeisterTask organizes and structures tasks and programs using colorful layouts. You can also use your dashboard to keep track of what's going on within your squad.

Pivot Tracker

Pivotal Tracker is yet another remote job app for tracking agile sprints and managing client projects. It is extremely common among developers all over the world.

TaskWorld

TaskWorld is a project management app similar to Trello or Asana. What distinguishes it is the addition of the chat feature. When planning your activities, keep in contact with the rest of the team.

10,000ft

10,000ft is a fantastic app that is ideal not just for a distributed workforce but also for teams in general. The visual interface, which looks like a prettier version of a Gantt map, aids in keeping track of things. It also helps you to monitor your time and generate reports that analyze the profitability of projects and jobs.

5. Productivity

Staying active can be one of the most difficult challenges for remote employees. There are too many possible distractions in your home office, and there are too many things to keep track of as a freelancer or entrepreneur. But don't worry! Here are some fantastic apps to help you get through the day.

TomatoTimer

You've most likely learned of the Pomodoro Technique. You divide your job into 25-minute sprints and take a 3-5-minute break in each working hour. This allows the brain to relax and regenerate fresh energy. The TomatoTimer does just that: it slows the clock and reminds you to take breaks.

Simplish

Simplish is a task management software that allows you to organize your tasks, take notes and thoughts, arrange activities and tasks in a built-in calendar, and collaborate with colleagues on shared tasks. The app's color palette has been chosen to help improve your mood, and you'll even receive optimistic regular affirmations to help keep you upbeat at work.

When working from home, organizing your responsibilities and activities in several different workspaces will help you contextualize your everyday tasks and strike an optimal work/life balance.

Furthermore, this software helps you to arrange both the tasks and activities you must complete alone and those you must complete with your team and all of this in whatever number of workspaces you need to complete your workflows. You will also be able to exchange to-dos with team members and communicate with them when working on joint projects directly from the app.

The Daily Planner feature provides a shortlist of your daily activities to help you concentrate on your goals on a daily basis.

Forest

Forest is an app that helps you stop your phone and remain focused on your job in a novel way by associating your self-control with the fate of a virtual tree that you must care for.

Plant a seed in the Forest app whenever you want to concentrate on work:

- The seed will expand as long as you do not play with your phone.
- The tree withers and dies if you exit the program.

If you hold your ground, your seed will eventually grow into a tree, and you will have a lush forest that represents how fruitful you are.

This application aims to inspire you to avoid scrolling through your social media feeds and start working with maximum focus by allowing you to:

- Compete with coworkers to see who can hold their phones down the longest.
- Plant a tree with coworkers to represent joint work.
- Unlock up to 30 different tree species (+ white noise sounds).
- Advance to unlock achievements and rewards

With the support of the Trees for the Future company, you can also fund the planting of a real tree anywhere in the world, allowing you to remain active and still helping the climate.

iDoneThis

When it comes to scattered teams and multiple time zones, daily check-in meetings can be difficult. The app iDoneThis allows you to monitor your everyday tasks without having to hold a meeting. At the end of the day, team members announce their work performance, and the next morning, everyone receives the information and has the opportunity to comment on the tasks.

NowDoThis

If all of those project management software and to-do lists are too complicated for your needs and you're searching for a simple app, NowDoThis might be the solution. Make a list of your tasks and check them off when you complete them. It's easy.

Nozbe

Have you ever heard of Nozbe? It's past time! Nozbe is a versatile software that falls somewhere between project management and efficiency. You should arrange your incoming assignments, prioritize them, and handle them so that you can complete your work efficiently and effectively.

RescueTime

Have you ever wondered how much time you spend every day on Facebook, Tinder, or simply checking your emails? RescueTime keeps track of everything and allows you to assess our productivity. If you want to restrict the amount of time you spend on those websites or activities, the app also allows you to do so.

Perdoo

Would you want to use the same device as Google, Uber, or Intel? Perdoo is a remote work tool that allows you to set, update, and track your personal goals, as well as the goals of your team and company. The aim is to achieve your key results to achieve your objective (OKR = Objectives and Key Results).

Todoist

Todoist is a task management app that allows you to identify all of your tasks in a simple list, assign due dates to each task, monitor your progress with them, and checkmark them when done.

What Nozbe can do for a team, Todoist can do for a person. You can add tasks by giving each one a summary. However, you can transform emails from coworkers or your supervisor to tasks and feedback as soon as you receive them. The browser extension also allows you to turn fascinating articles and websites that you encounter when browsing the web into tasks. You can set automatic, repeated deadlines for and type of task that will activate based on how long it took you to complete previous tasks of the same type.

6. Health

When you work from home, you don't drive around as much as you would if you worked in an office. You don't have to leave the house, go to the office, sprint between meeting rooms, or eat lunch in a cafeteria. Your body would most likely be dissatisfied with the lack of activity.

Another critical consideration is mental health. Trying to remain focused when working from home with all of the possible distractions can be difficult at times. The apps mentioned below may be of assistance.

Mindfulness
I'll never get tired of extolling the virtues of meditation. Just a few minutes per day are needed to re-energize your brain and re-establish your ability to concentrate. Mindfulness is a simple app that offers tones and guided meditations.

Seven

Seven is a very useful fitness app that challenges you to a fast yet intense 7-minute workout. Exercises alternate between cardio and power and can be completed in a short break from work.

If you work from home, you'll need to take breaks — and what better way to take a break than with a balanced workout? Seven will assist you in selecting from 200 tailor-made workouts and exercises to help you vary your training.

You'll also be able to choose from a variety of entertaining personal trainers, such as Drill Sergeant and Cheerleader, to help keep you motivated during your workouts.

Take a Break Please

It can be very tempting to work all day when you work from home and don't have to worry about breaks or workplace closing hours. A painful hunchback, dry eyes, and a stiff neck are common outcomes. Take a Break Please is a smartphone app that forces you to take breaks during the day. It is just for your benefit.

Tide

Tide, like Mindfulness, is a meditation app that provides you with soothing melodies, calm backgrounds, and inspiring quotes.

Stretching Exercise

This app will assist you in incorporating stretching into your everyday routine in order to alleviate muscle fatigue, relieve discomfort, increase flexibility, and relieve stress.

If you spend most of your day sitting at a desk, you can experience neck, back, and shoulder pain. These activities can be beneficial. - one lasts approximately 3 to 4 minutes.

EyeLeo

This app sends you notifications when it's time to rest your eyes. It dims your monitor and guides you through eye exercises. It also switches off the computer for the duration you specify, allowing you to take longer breaks.

7 Minute Workout

You don't need a lot of time at work to get in a decent workout. Seven minutes of high-intensity exercise will get your heart rate up and your attitude up. Seven Minute Workout is a free app that offers short everyday workouts that can be done at any time of day.

Yoga Pocket / Pocket Yoga Teacher

As the names indicate, pocket Yoga and Pocket Yoga Teacher are yoga companion applications that you can hold in your pocket. They replicate the feel of exercising in a real yoga studio by playing calming music while a soothing voice guides you through your yoga poses and demonstrates how to breathe properly.

Practicing brief yoga poses during work breaks is an ideal way to alleviate tension and relax — and these two apps ensure you dive into a ready-made yoga routine in a matter of minutes.

Pocket Yoga allows you to customize your practice, length, and difficulty level, as well as the "environment" you want to practice in — as you advance, you'll be able to unlock new, exciting "environments."

7. Miscellaneous

Of course, there are a plethora of other useful remote work apps available that do not fall into any of the previously listed categories. Here are a few of the strongest.

NordVPN

If you don't want to operate from your safe network at home and instead want to go to a nice café or coworking room, keep data security in mind! Use NordVPN to build a secure network and to operate safely from public WIFI connections.

FixMe.IT

FixMe.IT is an IT support platform that assists support teams in remotely resolving app problems experienced by users. However, you can effectively use this tool's remote desktop control options when working from home.

Since this program allows you to access even unattended remote computers, it's ideal if you've left some important documents on your office computer and want a safe, remote way to retrieve them from your home laptop.

It's also a good option if your coworkers ask you to access their own devices from afar for some reason. When working with a colleague, you'll also be able to share your own screen and conveniently move between different remote desktops you've accessed.

You will not only be able to obtain files from remote devices, but you will also be able to send them to remote devices when conducting live chats.

Bear

We're aware that Evernote and OneNote are excellent tools for keeping your daily notes secure and organized. Bear is an excellent option that allows you to take offline notes and thereby improve your productivity.

LastPass

LastPass remembers all of your passwords and usernames, so you don't have to. You can also share various access levels with your team members without revealing the actual password.

Noisli

Human brains are enthralling. While some people can only perform when the room is completely silent, others need a noisy environment to get them moving. Noisli creates synthetic noises such as wind in the forest or a crowded coffee shop. If you want to mask unwelcome sounds, there is a wide variety of white noise to choose from.

Timezone.io

You'll need a time zone app. It makes no difference which one. You MUST have one if your team, customers, or business partners are located all over the world. Timezone.io is a fantastic tool for seeing what time everybody is in and organizing meetings and deadlines.

Worldtime Buddy

World Time Buddy is a fast and easy tool for comparing various time zones at a glance. Simply pick the cities whose time zones you want to compare and drag the grid over the times.

This tool is ideal for when your remote team members are in a different time zone, which you can keep in mind when deciding on the best times to schedule meetings and collaborative work. Given that adjusting the clocks for Daylight Savings Time is an issue that many people ignore while preparing their workdays, this tool notifies you of such planned clock adjustments a day in advance.

Workfrom

You don't want to work from home today? Not a problem. Workfrom shows you the best cafès, bars, restaurants, or coworking spaces near you that have excellent WIFI, plenty of power outlets, and delicious food choices.

Are You Ready to Simplify Your Remote Work?

Oh my goodness, what a list! You don't need any of these remote work apps, of course. However, do yourself a favor and put a few to the test. Examine how you like the features and how they feel to you. If you like the idea and need the functions but aren't a fan of the design, try something else! There are several variations of everything on the market, only waiting for you to try them.

I'm confident you'll find one or more applications that are ideal for your needs and will make your work-from-home job easier.

WORK FROM HOME IDEAS

In recent years, there has been an increase of interest in jobs that allow you to work from home, not only from individuals but also from employers that see the advantages of developing positions that allow workers to work from home. According to an UpWork survey, by 2028, 73 percent of all departments would have remote workers—and this result came before COVID-19 pushed businesses to experiment with remote work on a large scale.

Both parties are finding that you do not need to be in the same geographic area or even in the same time zone as the workplace in many situations.

Parents, caregivers, and people with chronic illnesses and disabilities, as well as people searching for more flexible hours or the right to work from anywhere, are often looking for work-from-home opportunities. Some of these positions are part-time and could enable you to work with several clients at the same time, while others are full-time.

If you want to work from home, there are many opportunities available that require a wide range of skills and experience levels—and many of them pay wages equivalent to full-time, on-site employment.

Freelance Jobs to Do From Home

If you want a flexible schedule where you can set your own hours, work from home, and, yes, even work in your pajamas, a freelance job could be for you. A lot of work can now be done remotely, so your fantasies of working from home can come true.

1. Customer Care or Member Service Representative

Customer support representatives answer clients' questions, fix their issues, and assist them with orders over the phone or online, and it's one of the simplest work-from-home careers to get started in. Most entry-level reps earn around $12 per hour, while more seasoned reps earn around $15.50 per hour, with an hourly rate of $14. These roles, though, are not as adaptable as other work-from-home opportunities.

For example, if your shift runs from 8 a.m. to 5 p.m., you are supposed to be on call for the entire time.

2. Website Tester

Website testers evaluate the accuracy and usability of websites and web applications on various devices, including desktops, laptops, and handheld devices. Testers go to a website or use an app, perform a few activities, and then share their findings. They provide candid input on usability and clarification and their level of engagement with the content. The hourly rate is $25 on average. You can find jobs by registering with sites such as UserTesting, Userlytics, and StartUpLift.

3. Online Instructor

Online educators, like traditional teachers, offer instruction in particular subjects, organize lesson plans, and track student progress. Anyone with a teaching degree and a particular ability, such as fluency in a foreign language, is ideal for this role. You'll instruct a class using an online platform like Zoom or Google Meet. Positions range from kindergarten to 12th grade, as well as college and continuing education in all subject areas. Most jobs pay about $25 per hour, but one-on-one coaching will pay up to $100 to $200 per hour.

4. Virtual Assistant

Virtual assistants handle everything from appointment scheduling to analysis. Some jobs require only administrative duties such as managing calendars and schedules and invoicing customers, while others require copywriting and social media management expertise. Positions pay an average of $15 per hour, but candidates with public relations, writing and editing, and social media experience will earn up to $20 per hour. Most virtual assistants operate with several clients at once.

5. Captioner

Captioners transcribe pre-recorded audio and video, so being able to type quickly and accurately is necessary for this work. You may also sign up to caption live television shows, but many of those who do so have previously served as court reporters and use a stenotype system with a phonetic keyboard and special software to ensure accuracy. Captioners make an average of $14 per hour. You can search for employment through organizations like Rev and Upwork, or you can look for positions at specific companies like Caption Media Group or CaptionMax.

6. Transcriptionist

Transcriptionists listen to voice recordings and write them down. Medical and legal offices use transcriptionists to type out dictated notes from physicians and lawyers. Most companies need knowledge of medical terminology and procedures, as well as legal jargon. Beginning transcriptionists usually earn about $13 per hour, while more experienced transcriptionists typically earn about $20 per hour.

7. SEO Specialist

An SEO (search engine optimization) professional analyzes, evaluates and implements improvements to websites in order to increase the number of visitors and boost the site's ranking on search engines. Most positions require at least one year of experience and knowledge of industry SEO tools and techniques such as Google Analytics and website development platforms such as Squarespace. The average SEO specialist earns between $13 and $27 per hour.

8. Online Therapist

Online therapists provide real-time mental health support through digital platforms such as video conferencing, phone calls, and text messages. To practice online, you must have a master's degree in psychology or social work as well as an unrestricted license, so there is an initial investment. However, there is a growing demand for telehealth services that connect patients and healthcare providers. Most online therapists earn between $18 and $40 per hour.

9. Proofreader

A proofreader ensures that written text is error-free in terms of grammatical, spelling, punctuation, and formatting. Suppose you have good attention to detail and are familiar with the AP Stylebook and the Chicago Manual of Style. In that case, you will earn about $18 per hour proofreading for advertising agencies, websites, public relations companies, and textbook authors. This job is incredibly versatile, and you can complete it on your own time as long as you follow the deadline for proofreading the paper.

10. Survey Taker

A variety of companies will pay you to take surveys and send them your honest opinion on sports, movies, consumer goods, and other topics of general interest. Per a completed survey, you will be paid between $1 and $20. You may sign up for surveys with a variety of polling agencies, including 2020 Research.

11. Mobile Notary

A notary public certifies the proper execution of documents such as real estate transactions, powers of attorney, and prenuptial agreements as a representative of the state. If you are a public notary, you may also become a mobile notary who is registered, bonded, and insured. If you are uncomfortable welcoming strangers into your home, offer to meet them at their workplace, a hospital, or another place. The average hourly wage is $15, but most jobs pay between $10 and $24.

12. Online Bookkeeper

If you have experience invoicing customers, running payroll, and managing accounts, you can easily find a virtual bookkeeping job by contracting directly with a local business or signing up with an agency like Bookminders; many need a bachelor's degree in accounting and QuickBooks knowledge. Most virtual bookkeeping jobs pay between $16 and $21 per hour.

13. Medical Coder

You would need to become a Certified Professional Coder in order to correctly interpret a patient's medical chart, examine it, assess their diagnosis, and then categorize the diagnoses and medical procedures according to a national classification system that allows doctors to submit medical claims to insurers. The average hourly wage is about $18.50. To find work, you might contract with a local physician's office or contact the American Association of Professional Coders or the American Health Information Management Association.

14 Consultant in Marketing

If you have expertise in digital marketing or branding, you will assist businesses in developing organized campaigns that use SEO, email marketing, social media, and other tools. The hourly rate for most jobs ranges from around $14 to $102 per hour, depending on your experience and track record as a marketer.

15. Web Developer

More and more technology firms are relocating jobs from the workplace to versatile or remote positions. If you have a bachelor's degree in computer science or a similar area, have completed a boot camp program, or have other equivalent programming experience, you might be able to find full-time job openings that provide flexible or remote work locations. The hourly wage ranges from $12 to $44.

Telehealth Nurse

Telehealth had been increasing in popularity before the coronavirus reached the United States, and it has seen an increase in demand as the healthcare system has been inundated with people who were hesitant to visit their doctor's office during the pandemic. Some employers are searching for full-time telehealth nurses to answer questions about COVID-19, but there are also part-time positions available. Just make sure to review the state's licensing standards to ensure you're eligible to work there. As a result, candidates who are licensed in more than one state could be especially appealing to recruiters. The hourly wage ranges from $19 to $42.

17. Translator

Depending on the job, these staffs translate the written or spoken word. At CyraCom, you can answer phones and assist people in contacting physicians, insurance companies, and even 9-1-1 operators. Translate.com allows you to work on a gig-by-gig basis, giving you more versatility. Just keep in mind that all gigs are first come, first served, and can cost as little as a penny per word. The hourly wage ranges from $10 to $35.

18. Writer

Do you enjoy playing with words? If you're a novice writer or a seasoned pro, the ability to put sentences together will land you a work-from-home job in a variety of industries. Of course, the more experience you have, the more money you will make. Expertise in a specific area, such as sports, parenting, personal finance, technology, or science, may also help improve your prospects and narrow your job search.

In addition to the full-time positions currently available at Contently and NerdWallet, you should browse the various freelance writer work pages, such as ProBlogger.com, nDash, and Scripted. You should also try pitching proposals to newspapers, magazines, and other media directly. The hourly wage ranges from $10 to $50.

19. Sales Agent

The salesman is not dead; he is simply working from home. Companies in a variety of sectors, from finance to technology to health care, are searching for top salespeople with varying degrees of expertise (and, if appropriate, a sales license) to push their goods and services from a remote location. Some higher-level positions might also be responsible for managing a sales team. Many of the opportunities can necessitate travel once COVID-19 restrictions are eased further.

The average hourly wage ranges from $10 to $20. (insurance sales agent).

20. Fundraising Coordinator

Contribute to the funding of causes in which you believe. You may get a full-time entry-level job that allows you to interact directly with potential or current donors. If you have the necessary experience, you might be able to land a more senior-level role that needs proven grant writing and fundraising plan creation skills. The hourly wage ranges from $10 to $20.

Tips for Landing a Work-From-Home Job

The application process is becoming more dynamic as more people pursue flexible hours and roles. There are also online scams masquerading as work-from-home opportunities to be wary of. Here's what you need to do to get a remote job while avoiding scams:

Apply Right Away

The trick to landing one of these work-from-home opportunities is to apply as soon as the vacancy is released. It is not uncommon for 100 to 150 people to respond to an ad within the first hour of its publication.

Improve Your Work-from-Home Capabilities gleam

Employees who work from home must be self-motivated and self-starters. So, when you apply, make sure to emphasize those qualities and any other soft skills that demonstrate the ability to function independently. Call attention to your ability to keep track of your own productivity and to ask for support proactively, he says. For example, in your cover letter, you might say, "When faced with a dilemma, I search out solutions rather than waiting for the issue to solve itself," and then provide an example.

While many applicants for work-from-home jobs are caregivers and parents, there is no need to concentrate on this when responding to job postings. Instead, emphasize why you are the right person for the job from the company's standpoint. Companies recruit remotely because they can't find the talent locally, they want to save money or need someone who is incredibly good at their work.

So, if you're applying to be a web developer, your application should express that you're the best web developer they can employ and justify why, according to him. For example, your letter may state, "I've created more than 50 websites for a wide range of clients, and I can turn projects around quickly with minimal supervision and guidance."

Avoid Scams

Before applying for a job, make certain that it is a valid role with a real organization. Even if you've never heard of the brand, you should be able to find information about it and read reviews about it online. In other words, you want to ensure that the company has a digital presence that extends beyond what they build themselves (like a LinkedIn page or website).

Most importantly, you should never have to pay money to apply for a job or start working. Make sure you understand how and how much you will be billed, he advises. Often, trust your instincts. If anything does not sound good, do not proceed with the position.

Best Freelance Websites to Find Job

Freelancing is a fascinating practice. You want to jump right in and start making money as soon as you learn about it. But wait, before you begin, you must first learn the answers to some very important questions, such as what are the available platforms for freelancing, which one best suits you, and so on. While there are no fixed guidelines for freelancing, it is always a good idea to become acquainted with the various freelancing platforms' rules, specifications, and responsibilities.

This article recommends the top three freelancing sites that are well recognized and often used. These are the best freelancing sites available. They all have their own smartphone apps as well. Although some people use several freelancing platforms simultaneously, it is recommended that as a novice, you choose one platform to begin with. When you have a strong presence on one platform, conquering others would be a breeze.

Fiverr

Background

Fiverr, which debuted in 2010, is the world's largest digital services freelancing site. It was based on the idea of creating a digital marketplace where everyone could buy and sell services. It allows sellers to sell services in their field of expertise and buyers to search the list of freelancers who provide such services and place orders.

Services Included

The site's key service categories include writing, translation, graphic design, video editing, and programming. Each service provided is referred to as a "Gig."

Earnings

Earning money on Fiverr starts at $5 and can reach thousands of dollars with extra gigs. It's worth noting that all sales up to and including $40 are subject to a $2 service charge, and all purchases above $40 are subject to a 5% service fee.

In short, when you start selling on Fiverr, $2 will be deducted from your earnings per gig to compensate Fiverr for providing you with the site.

Pros of Selling on Fiverr
- Easy Selling

It is truly simple to sell products on Fiverr! It takes less than ten minutes to create an account. It is easy to use. You must update your profile, add a bank account, verify for auto-transfer, create some nice descriptive Gigs, and get started. If you are dedicated to delivering outstanding service, you will make a living.

- Fiverr Seller Tiers

Fiverr Seller Levels allow you to be rewarded for your work by moving up the Fiverr tier scale for exceptional work. The level-up provides you with increased exposure and a service upgrade package that allows you to completely customize your bid, which was previously available for $5.

- Make Money Doing What You Do

People who work as freelancers will earn thousands of dollars a month. You can receive far more than a normal job employee if you are a committed worker who works with discipline and passion.

How does it work?

- Register and Create A Gig

Sign up for free, create a gig, and sell your work to a global audience. You must build your gigs professionally and deliver the best prices possible. You may have to lower the price at first to gain an audience and some constructive feedback, but that's okay. Take a few skills tests as well to demonstrate to prospective employers that you are eligible for the job. Some gigs, such as writing, require you to take exams, which will be shown to you before publishing your gig.

- Produce Excellent Work

Look for buyer inquiries and give your deals to them. When you receive an order, you will be informed, and you will use the device contact channel to share information with the customers. Respond to requests as soon as possible, and always deliver work on time or before the deadline. The sooner you start, the better. If you are late for submission for obvious reasons, it is always best to tell your client beforehand in a professional manner, and they will gladly approve your request.

- Get Paid

Payment is transferred to you upon fulfillment of the order. When it's time to turn in the project, you will request a five-star review and ranking for your efforts.

Earning Money Without Having Skills

If you lack creativity and expertise, you can still make money on Fiverr in two ways:

- Learning skill-based courses available on the Fiverr marketplace: When you finish a course, it automatically appears on your Fiverr profile. Since you know the issue, you can now sell the service with authority.
- Become a Fiverr partner and recommend Fiverr gigs to other companies: Having a blog as well as a social profile on LinkedIn and Instagram can help with this.

Fiverr Pro

Fiverr Pro is an updated version of Fiverr that is available for certified, experienced sellers who want to meet the needs of Fiverr business buyers. It doesn't matter if you're new to Fiverr or a seasoned seller; as long as you're a talented freelancer on Fiverr, you can apply.

Upwork

Background

Upwork, formerly known as Elance-oDesk, is a global freelancing website where companies and individuals can interact to do business. Elance-oDesk was rebranded as Upwork in 2015. Their headquarters are in California, USA. Upwork Global Inc. is the full name of the platform.

Upwork is the world's second-largest freelance marketplace, with three million jobs posted annually worth a total of $1 billion.

Services included

Upwork provides the same resources like Fiverr, with the key categories being publishing, translation, graphic design, video editing, and programming.

"Connects" are tokens used by freelancers on Upwork to upload applications and apply for jobs. Each new application needs 1 to 5 connects (zero if invited or rehired by a client).

Earning

You are paying by the hour on hourly contracts, making this a preferred choice when your project needs flexibility. You are paying a set sum for a project deliverable or set of deliverables under a fixed-price contract.

Upwork also charges a service fee to freelancers depending on the cumulative amount billed to a single customer. You pay 20% for the first $500 you charge your client across all contracts, 10% for total payments with your client between

$500.01 and $10,000, and 5% for total payments with your client above $10,000.

Pros of Selling on Upwork

• Simplified Hiring

When you complete your profile, Upwork will recommend suitable jobs to you. Upwork's advanced algorithms illustrate projects for which you are an excellent fit. You can also look for projects and respond to client invitations on your own.

• High-Rating and Emerging Talent Programs

Benefit from increased exposure as a result of the inclusion of prestigious programs.

• Work on a significant project with a high-profile client

The pricing structure of Upwork allows clients to return. You can easily obtain long-term contracts from your existing customers. Get repeat and referral company. The greater your performance on previous assignments, the more likely it is that new clients will recruit you on Upwork.

• Various Payment Options

Upwork handles both invoices and payments. Expect a straightforward and streamlined procedure. Choose a payment system that works best for you, such as direct deposit or PayPal, as well as wire transfer and other options.

• Projects on an hourly or fixed-price basis

Send timesheets via Upwork for hourly work. Set milestones and funds are released via Upwork escrow features for fixed-price projects.

How does it work?

• Register and Choose a Membership Plan

First, you must register. Then choose the membership package that best meets your requirements. You can still upgrade or downgrade your membership package at any time.

• Build Your Profile Fill out as many fields as possible to build a profile highlighting your expertise. Extend on your experience and show your preferred hourly rate. Profiles on Upwork will not be available until they have been completed and tested. You may also take a few qualifications tests to demonstrate to prospective clients that you have the necessary skills.

• Configure Your Payment Method

To be paid, notify Upwork of your preferred method of payment. There are two different methods for transferring funds, and you can use either one or both of them. It is recommended that both be set up.

• Make use of Upwork Messages

When you use Messages on Upwork, collaboration becomes a breeze. Organize and organize conversations, connect with clients in real-time, and sync and exchange deliverables.

Earning without Skills

You can still earn money on Upwork even if you don't have any skills or experience by performing tasks like writing reviews, making on-demand comments, typing, translating, and so on. You will still learn new skills along the way. Doing these small jobs will help you learn how to work with your customers, how to take orders, verify payment methods, what to say to a customer, and so on.

Upwork membership scheme

Upwork basic membership is free and includes all of the features you'll need to use Upwork for your company. Upwork, on the other hand, provides a paying Freelancer Plus membership option for those seeking additional premium benefits. It provides Upwork Payment Security, plus ten additional Connects per month (for a total of 70), the right to carry over up to 70 unused Connects to the next monthly billing period, the freedom to buy extra Connects, and insight into what others are bidding on the deal.

Freelancer

Historical context

Freelancer is a crowdsourcing marketplace platform based in Australia that was created in 2009. It enables prospective employers to post-work, which freelancers can then bid on. The company's headquarters are in Sydney, Australia.

Services Included

They are offering all of the utilities that are available on other websites. The Jobs page contains over 750 job categories, and you can almost certainly find one that suits your skills. Website Development, Graphic Design, Logo Design, Marketing, Writing, and Mobile App are the most common. These services are usually sold at a high cost.

Earning

This is determined by the form of membership you have. The fee for fixed-price ventures is approximately 10%, or $5.00 (at least 3 percent). For freelancers employed on supported or chosen projects, there is a 15% charge.

In addition to the above, you should be aware that on "normal" projects, you pay a 10% fee when you approve an awarded project, not when you are paid.

On the supported project with an invitation, you pay a 15% charge when you accept a project, not when you are compensated for the work.

Bidding is completely open.

Pros of Selling on Freelancer
- Job Availability

Outsourcing is one way for employers to expand their business without investing too much money on items like supplies, office space, and so on. One of Freelancer.com's selling points is getting the job done for less money, so more employers are persuaded to post jobs on the web. Freelancer.com offers lower quotes on most work, which helps the employer; thus, more companies use freelancer.com when trying to outsource a job.

- Time Management Using a Time Tracker

One of the benefits of working as a freelancer is the ability to work from home. Time-Tracker is a tool on Freelancer.com. The app's time monitoring is mostly used for tracking hourly projects. The employee manages the app, who can then take screenshots of the hours worked to send to the employer as evidence.

- Costs

Via their bids, freelancers may specify how much they want to be paid. When working for a job with a fixed payment, freelancers can opt to be paid hourly or by defined milestones.

- Round-the-clock assistance

Their support group is made up of real people who are available 24 hours a day, seven days a week.

How does it work?
- Create Your Profile and Sign Up

Create an account. Make a full and presentable profile that includes your personality, resume, portfolio, and skills. Certain projects demand that your profile represents specific skills, so the more you list, the more opportunities you will get.

- Locate Projects and Begin Bidding

Go to the Jobs or Competitions page to find the tasks and contests you want to work on. You'll find appropriate projects available for bidding on the jobs side. In the case of competitions, you submit an entry.

Before submitting your bid, write a convincing argument why the employer should choose you over anyone else.

- Reach an agreement and get to work.

Come to an understanding with the employer on the project scope, deadlines, and milestone bonuses, and establish a signed agreement to seal the contract. After that, get to work. To communicate with your boss, use the built-in chatbox. Maintain a responsible schedule, budget, and contact.

- Get Paid And Earn Five-Star Feedback

After submitting a good project, you will be paid and able to withdraw your funds through PayPal Wire Transfer, Moneybookers, or your designated local bank account. By submitting high-quality, employer-satisfied work, you will earn a five-star rating. Positive feedback is often a valuable asset to your portfolio.

Earning Money Without Having Skills

There are several career types on Freelancer.com.

- Determine the field in which you have any expertise.
- Begin bidding on its operation if there is enough demand for it.
- Determine your keywords and audience.
- Deliver something valuable for free as part of the quote.

This should be about 10% of the total contract value and must be beneficial to the consumer.

- Bid on a large number of jobs and work hard on your CRO (Conversion Rate Optimization).
- Deliver quickly and with high quality.
- Increase your revenue by adding more items or upselling.
- Plan for Freelancer Membership

Use membership enhancements such as the Annual Plus Membership to help you gain more by receiving more bids each month, increasing your job volume and thus profits.

In conclusion

Freelancing is a fantastic business model that helps you to get started with almost no overheads by putting in a little time and enthusiasm. However, to stand out among other gigs, a great deal of hard work and research is needed. It's a good idea to invest in a small freelancing course before embarking on your journey, so you know what to expect.

How to Ask Your Boss to Work From Home

So far, we've seen the jobs you can do from home as a freelancer, but what if you already have a good job and want to leave the office to work from home?

If you want to work from home, you should develop a strategy for approaching your boss. Decide on the type of schedule you want and what would fit best for both you and your business.

When negotiating a work-from-home contract, be prepared to be versatile. The more flexibility you recommend to your boss, the more likely it is that you will receive a "yes" response.

Prepare Your Case

Create a case focused on business requirements.

Working from home will help you save money, reduce your commute, and improve your work-life balance. However, do not begin with the benefits to you. Begin by detailing the company's gains. Highlight cost savings, efficiency gains, and other aspects in which working from home can assist the company in meeting its objectives.

Understand the company's policies.

Your company may already have a structured telecommuting program in place, in which case you should be aware of it before meeting with your boss. Remember what you've seen in the workplace if the employee handbook doesn't specifically mention flexible work opportunities. Do other workers work from home, and if so, who, how much, and how does it work?

In your conversations with your boss, do not bring up any staff. Keep the conversation focused on your situation and how working from home will help the team.

Make a proposal
Writing a telecommuting plan outlining how you can comfortably operate from home can assist your boss in making a case for you. In reality, you should put your request in writing before your meeting. That way, your boss isn't taken aback by your appeal, and you're prepared to explain why you don't need to spend all of your working hours at the office.

Make use of sample letters to help you form your order.
When requesting to work from home, it is usually better to speak with your supervisor in person. On the other hand, templates and examples will help you organize your thoughts and plan to make your case. Before you write your own, look over sample letters for working from home.

Request a Meeting

Ask for a meeting to discuss the matter.

Don't take your boss by surprise with an offer to work from home. Schedule a meeting ahead of time, and make sure you choose a time when your boss is likely to be open to hearing your ideas. (In other words, don't make your request during your team's busiest season or when things are otherwise busier than usual.)

Prepare to resolve any issues that could arise.
You can need to assuage your boss's fears before receiving approval, particularly if telecommuting is not widely used at your business. Your boss may be worried about efficiency, connectivity, or team morale. Prepare your responses and keep in mind that you intend to persuade — don't be defensive or rely on emotional appeals.

Demonstrate Your Availability
Provide evidence that you will be available. Commit to being visible, communicative, and available. Depending on how the team communicates, this could mean being on Slack from 9 a.m. to 5 p.m. every day, emailing the manager with progress updates at regular times, or being available for Zoom chats regularly.

Be adaptable.

Request a trial period.
Maybe you'll work from home every Friday for the rest of the quarter or twice a week for the next month or two and then reevaluate. Set deliverables targets and suggest a trial period that works for your team and business.

Be prepared to wait for a response.
Remember that your manager will not be willing to permit you during your meeting. Your manager should need to

consult with their supervisor and/or the company's Human Resources Department.

THE WORK-FROM-HOME MINDSET

The short-term shift to remote working last year has gradually become a more permanent, fundamental change in the way we work.

Shifting to a Remote Mindset

The difficulties associated with remote work may be deceptive: If you've recently left an office job, it might seem that the best thing to do is to try to replicate all of the memories that come with working in an office. Being remote, however, is not the same as sharing physical space. Instead of duplicating the in-office setting, we must adapt—or even completely rethink—those interactions for the distributed background.

Being able to distill our experiences and focus on what we value is what remote thinking entails. What aspects of working in an office are most important to us? How can we remove these components and repurpose them for use in distributed teams? If we've identified the most important outcomes of the in-office experience, we can start replicating them in a remote environment.

Ask good questions, provide good answers

The remote work model necessitates that we are careful and accurate. Consider asking a colleague sitting across from you a question about a part of the codebase you're unfamiliar with. This setup enables you to share questions and answers in real-time, as well as clarify your reasoning. They might end the conversation by referring to some documentation. If, for example, your coworker is 10 hours ahead of you, this rapid-fire, synchronous sharing of information does not work nearly as well. Although time zone variations are just one aspect of the remote experience, if you both respond during your working hours, the exchange could take a week.

In the absence of automatic peer reviews, we must think critically about what questions we pose and how we ask them. A well-considered, well-thought-out query that offers context and knowledge on what you know, what you don't know, and what ideas you've already considered would yield a more valuable response than a question that necessitates additional follow-up. Learning how to ask one good question instead of a set of less successful ones will help bridge time zones, recreating the feeling of getting someone instantly available to provide context and help you get unstuck.

The same rules apply to providing a well-formed and well-considered response. A good question, like a good answer, gives as much context as possible upfront. A good answer clearly states any assumptions you might have about how someone addresses an issue from the start. Answering a question entails describing why something is happening as well as figuring out how to fix it. A good response also allows the use of previously written things, such as internal and external documents, code fragments, and old pull requests, to help provide context.

Consider the appropriate tooling.

When supported by the proper tools, effective communication will go much further. Smaller, in-office teams can have behaviors that are dependent on co-location. For example, a previous team I worked on would announce—out loud—when they were deploying major releases or rolling back a shift. It worked in our sense at the time, but it is not scalable and does not provide visibility for remote team members. When the entire team is remote, every message is deposited into some communication channel, resulting in a lot to sift through. I've discovered that it's beneficial to strike a balance between drowning in too much detail and coping with a lack of it. Translating in-office announcements into a Whatsapp channel for team announcements will provide quick access to real-time information for a small enough team. This approach worked well for our team of less than 20, but for larger teams, some curation might be required — important announcements may need to be tailored to those working on various products or using different sections of the technology stack.

Often the results we want from an encounter are a little hazier. How do you assess momentum when you can't tell if the team is making progress or is stuck? My mornings in an office were organized around 30-minute stand-ups, during which the team exchanged status updates, flagged blockers, and requested pairing time. The synchronous aspect of stand-ups, however, does not always translate when teams work remotely. There are a few different methods you might take. One basic tactic that I've found to be useful is to set an automatic reminder to ping the team at the same time every day with the same questions: What did you work on yesterday? What are you going to focus on today? Are you obstructed? Do you wish to pair up?

My current dispersed team gained a much clearer understanding of what everyone was working on when using this scheduled reminder to touch base. Personally, I felt more linked to my colleagues and better prepared to support them as a leader: I could calibrate our productivity more effectively, determine who was stuck or in need of help, and recognize when we were blocked enough that I needed to bring in additional support or resources. Since then, other teams in our organization have followed this workflow, and my team has extended our automated tooling by incorporating new integrations and reminders. I haven't had to worry about putting together a team update for our weekly all-hands meetings in months since we have a bot that reminds us to thread our updates. Small changes to everyday procedures will reduce the number of routine activities that everyone on a team must remember to do.

Adapt and prosper

Every team can develop their own ideas, and reconsidering the default will lead to more innovative and successful results.

Not every component of a physical world has a simple remote analog, nor can every solution be conveniently automated. Effective communication with those we work most closely with necessitates a number of touchpoints and subtleties that are difficult to nail down—even in person. But, before we give up, consider what results of a healthy relationship with a colleague are truly important. We can change our experiences to prioritize certain outcomes once we've identified the nature of what nourishes a thriving coworker relationship.

A younger engineer, for example, may be searching for new experiences, a comfortable place to ask questions, career advice, daily input from a trusted confidant, and even an advocate. In my current team, this takes the form of several weekly pairing sessions between younger and more seasoned engineers and careful, proactive project scoping to ensure that new engineers aren't working on anything that is too far beyond their capabilities. A nice side effect of this scoping strategy has been the effect it has had on the rest of the team: Tasks became more established, and projects with the potential for collaboration and learning became more apparent. As a result, engineers at all levels have well-defined deliverables and a straightforward path to being better at partnering and training their peers, if they wish.

The seemingly insignificant experiences of day-to-day workplace life have their own outcomes. By refocusing on the nature of these experiences, we will find distant ways to make the most of them. Instead of asking how to duplicate team happy hours, we should ask ourselves how to communicate with our coworkers. Instead of asking what to do in place of group lunches, we should consider how we can have ways for team members to get to know one another better. Every team can come up with their own ideas, and reconsidering the default will lead to more innovative and successful results.

Shifting to a remote mentality does not imply abandoning team building. It just takes a change in perspective — away from what the experiences look like in an office setting and toward what those interactions actually resulted in and how you can produce equally satisfying outcomes in a remote setting.

Maintaining the Growth Mindset

The transition has been more difficult than many of us expected for many of us who have started working from home in recent weeks. We are not only thrown out of our daily routine but we are also confronted with a whole new set of problems in our new work climate. The best way to deal with the challenges of being stuck at home is to cultivate a healthy growth mentality, and today we'll share four keys to help you succeed.

There is a major risk that workers will lose motivation when most firms move to work-from-home, small shifts, or other changed work routines. When we lose the constant affirmation, it can be difficult to remain motivated and connected to our work. Many workers complain that the isolation and lack of routine have a detrimental effect on their mental health, and the disadvantages will compound if the quarantine continues longer.

A growth mentality will protect you from setbacks. Anyone can develop a growth mindset, but it can be especially beneficial to those of us adapting to this new work-life balance and the financial instability that may lie ahead.

What exactly is a growth mindset?

A growth mindset assumes that one's skills and talents can be developed through hard work and persistence. A growth mentality implies that you accept ownership and responsibility for your situation and its future outcomes. Individuals with a growth mentality are willing to try new things, overcome challenges, and recover from mistakes because they understand that this is where change will take root.

A fixed mindset is a polar opposite of a development mindset, in which you assume that your talents and abilities are fixed and cannot be changed or improved. A fixed mentality restricts your ability to react to challenges and can leave you feeling inefficient and unequal to the hiccups you'll encounter when stuck at home or adapting to the "new standard."

Why do I need a growth mentality right now?

There is a major risk that workers will lose motivation when most firms move to work-from-home, small shifts, or other changed work routines. When we lose the constant affirmation, it can be difficult to remain motivated and connected to our work. Many workers complain that their mental health suffers as a result of their loneliness and lack of routine, and the disadvantages can escalate as the condition worsens.

A growth mentality will protect you from setbacks. Anyone can develop a growth mindset, but it can be especially beneficial to those of us adapting to this new work-life balance and the financial instability that may lie ahead.

Tips for maintaining a growth mindset

1. Acknowledge the struggle

It's easy to neglect or minimize the difficulties you're experiencing in your current job routine. It can even be difficult to pinpoint the causes of your "off" feelings. However, one secret to developing a growth mentality is to embrace the obstacles that lie ahead of you.

Don't be afraid to mention the obstacles to your productivity, mindset, overall mental health, family life, and any other areas that this transition is affecting. Maintaining a work-life balance, focusing while you have children in your "office," insufficient workspace conditions, and other factors can all significantly slow you down.

Recognizing the mountains makes climbing them easier, and problem-solving is more likely to be successful. Consider your specific challenges as opportunities to strengthen yourself or learn something new.

2. Dream big

Spend some time imagining the perfect scenario and consequences of being stranded at home. Consider the resources you now have that you may not have had in the workplace and how you should take advantage of them.

What does your perfect work-from-home day entail? How do you incorporate stuff you like and desire into your current situation?

Some suggestions for designing the ideal work-from-home lifestyle include:

- Spending more time communicating with your family
- Dressing in your favorite casual and comfortable clothing • Working outdoors or going on walks for breaks
- Cooking your favorite meals Enjoying your favorite form of entertainment while working (music, television, movies, podcasts)
- Participating in a virtual conference from the comfort of your sofa
- Adjusting your work hours to allow for sleeping in or a midday nap
- Completing a large project that impresses your boss.

Most business leaders want to protect their workers through these shifts in the workplace. We would be wise to prioritize our own well-being.

3. **Set** *objectives*

Working from home can cause us to lose track of time. Since we don't have the daily cycles of a workplace to prompt self-assessment, we can find ourselves working on a project for much longer than required. A lack of transparency can also lead to lower productivity and self-esteem. By setting goals with a development mentality, you can arm yourself against these problems.

Setting deadlines, has become obvious to me as being critical for home-based staff, like myself, because it not only gives you a time frame for completing your assignments but, most importantly, keeps you focused.

Divide your goals into timeframes that work for you, such as goals before lunch, regular goals, and weekly goals. To maximize transparency, write them down or share them virtually with your team. Goals serve as a reminder to yourself that development, change, and achievement are still possible, even if you're in your PJs for the fifth day in a row.

4. Visualize
It's time to rise.

Nobody knows when the new sanctions will be lifted or what the state of the economy will be when we emerge from this crisis. Our only assurance is our own effort and mindset within our own spheres of influence. We will overcome the obstacles of working from home, social distancing, quarantines, and economic ramifications through cultivating a growth mindset.

What are the Psychological Effects of Working from Home?

Have you found a difference in your mental health when you started working from home? Do you feel more tired because you don't have to commute? Do you experience feelings of loneliness even though you can clock in and out from anywhere you want?

Work-from-home jobs can be taxing on your mental health. It can turn usually upbeat, active worker bees into drained, unmotivated, irritable toads.

So, before you reach rock bottom, learn how to recognize the symptoms of deteriorating mental health so you can plan the next steps.

The three most widely mentioned problems that remote staff and digital nomads face are as follows:

Isolation and loneliness
When you don't have to go somewhere for work, you could go for days without speaking to someone.

While you avoid annoying colleagues while you work remotely, you do miss the social aspect of chatting and venting about work and life. This camaraderie does not translate as well over Slack.

This disconnect from colleagues and the rest of the world can leave you feeling lonely and isolated. Loneliness is also linked to increased rates of depression, anxiety, and somatic symptoms such as random pain.

Stress, Anxiety, and Pressure

Working from home anxiety manifests itself in a variety of ways, including:

There is constant pressure to hustle. Do you have to look for work and then make it? You most likely work whenever you can. However, if you don't take time to disconnect and unplug, you risk burning out.

For people who work and sleep in the same room, the line between work and home life blurs. You may feel compelled to stay on when you should be off.

Wearing many hats causes stress. Working from home necessitates time management, invoicing skills, marketing, IT troubleshooting, customer care, and a variety of other skills. Switching between these hats many times a day would tire everyone out.

Depression

When you feel trapped at work, you can experience work from home depression. You may not feel like you're doing as well as your colleagues if you don't have a new nameplate on your desk or a fancy corner office.

Working from home can trigger anxiety, stress, and isolation, leading to or worsening depression.

Depression is more than just feeling down. According to psychological research, signs of depression include:

- Angry outbursts, irritability, or frustration (often over minor issues)
- Loss of interest or happiness in activities such as sex or hobbies
- Sleep disturbances, including insomnia and excessive sleeping
- Tiredness and lack of energy, making even simple tasks difficult
- Increased food cravings
- Anxiety, agitation, and restlessness
- Difficulty thinking, concentrating, making decisions, and remembering things

The good news is that working from home does not have to be detrimental to your mental health.

Taking care of your mental wellbeing is just as critical as exercising and consuming nutritious foods.

First and foremost, it is acceptable not to be okay. Respect where you are, whatever that might be.

Second, understand that you have the ability to enjoy a happier brain by making a few changes, as discussed in Chapter 3. Following such suggestions will protect your mental health from the isolation, anxiety, and depression that many remote workers experience.

If you are suffering from depression or anxiety, talk to someone you trust, consult your doctor, or seek the help of mental health professional. You're not by yourself. Know that tomorrow is still a new day.

CONCLUSION

While working from home inevitably comes with challenges, there are many benefits too, such as easy school pick-ups, fitting in exercise, being home for deliveries – even getting time to marinate a chicken for dinner. As a result, the proportion of remote employees is increasing year after year, with nearly half of global companies providing some kind of work-from-home alternative. Many workers value the flexibility and convenience that remote work offers.

As we saw in Chapter 2, you may have also found yourself among those saving a lot of money a year in commuting and other incidental costs, such as a fancy coffee every morning. If you are able, take the opportunity to stash this money into a savings account.

But adjusting to working from home if you're used to being in an office environment isn't always a walk in the park. Feeling disconnected from their coworkers, some people struggle to maintain their usual productivity level and communicate efficiently with their company.

I hope this book has provided you all the tools and knowledge you need to approach working from home with confidence and peace of mind. Now you know how to adapt to working from home: Use all this information to be productive and make the most of this exceptional opportunity that technological progress has given us. Good luck!

www.ingramcontent.com/pod-product-compliance
Lightning Source LLC
Chambersburg PA
CBHW070109120526
44588CB00032B/1398